OPEN HOUSE

CONVERSATIONS WITH LEIGH HATCHER

Also by Leigh Hatcher

I'm Not Crazy, I'm Just a Little Unwell

Open House: A new era with Leigh Hatcher

OPEN HOUSE

CONVERSATIONS WITH LEIGH HATCHER

WITH LINDY CHAMBERLAIN-CREIGHTON, MICHAEL CHAMBERLAIN RICK WARREN, LYNNE MCGRANGER, COLIN BUCHANAN, STEVE BIDDULPH TOMMY EMMANUEL, PETER JENSEN, KEN DUNCAN, REBECCA ST JAMES AND MANY MORE.

STRAND PUBLISHING
Sydney

Open House: Conversations with Leigh Hatcher

First published 2013 by Strand Publishing

The Open House radio program is a production of Hope Media Ltd:
www.hope1032.com.au

ISBN: 978-1-921202-87-2

Distributed in Australia by:
KI Entertainment
Unit 31, 317–321 Woodpark Rd
Smithfield NSW 2164 Australia
Phone: (02) 9604 3600
Fax: (02) 9604 3699
Email: sales@kientertainment.com.au
Web: www.kientertainment.com.au

Photograph of Rebecca St John courtesy of Provident Label Group
Cover photographs courtesy of David Oliver

Edited by Owen Salter
Cover design by Joy Lankshear
Typeset by Midland Typesetters, Maryborough, Australia
Printed by McPherson's Printing Group

Contents

Introduction vii

Lynne McGranger *'Irene Roberts' in* Home and Away 1
Justin Gardiner *From 'Underbelly' to church minister* 9
Lopez Lomong *Sudanese refugee, US Olympian* 17
Patricia Weerakoon *Eros, intimacy and the mind of God* 25
Mark Scott *ABC Managing Director* 33
Rick Warren *Author of* The Purpose Driven Life 41
Ann Fogarty *Ash Wednesday bushfire survivor* 49
Baroness Caroline Cox *Member of the House of Lords, founder of HART* 59
Colin Buchanan *Songwriter, performer* 67
Eric Metaxas *Dietrich Bonhoeffer's biographer* 75
Sheridan Voysey '*Resurrection Year*' 85
Tim Dixon *Political minder and social activist* 97
John Ortberg *Who is this man Jesus?* 107
Judith Durham *The voice of the Seekers* 117
Kay and Russell Clark *In the face of death* 125
Lindy Chamberlain-Creighton *Forgiveness* 135
Michael Chamberlain *Father of Azaria Chamberlain* 145
Rebecca St James *Singer, author, actress* 155

June Dally Watkins *Deportment and style queen* 163
Ralph Winter *Veteran Hollywood producer* 173
Peter Jensen *Former Anglican Archbishop of Sydney* 181
Tony Hoang *Former gang member, drug addict and dealer* 191
Will Graham *Evangelist and grandson of Billy Graham* 201
Michael Cassidy *Founder of African Enterprise* 209
Benny Perez *Founder of the Church of South Las Vegas* 219
Tommy Emmanuel *Guitar supremo* 227
Steve Biddulph *'Raising Girls'* 235
Richard Gill *Conductor, educator, maestro* 243
Sam Childers *'Machine Gun Preacher'* 253
Ken Duncan *Panoramic prince* 261

About Leigh Hatcher 269
About *Open House* 271

Introduction

I never cease to be amazed at the truly remarkable people, their absorbing stories and the thought-provoking issues we have on *Open House* across Australia every Sunday night.

At the beginning of the last two years I had a quiet private panic. Maybe we'd had all the best guests on already and the well would be empty for the coming year! Pretty soon my mind eased. The big names and the great stories just keep on coming. In fact, it's been a gusher—our cup continues to run over!

With this, the fifth *Open House* book, I'm absolutely convinced it lifts the bar even higher. I'm enormously grateful to the thirty people who have kindly agreed to be part of it.

This is a very challenging time to present a program like *Open House* with its aim of exploring 'life, faith and culture'. There's a growing hostility in the public square towards Christian faith. There's a widespread, entirely understandable dismay at the church's past actions and behaviour. The Christian voice is increasingly marginalised—or silenced.

Open House is well known as a program that's prepared to take on the hard questions and tough issues that confront Christian faith in today's world.

Yet as this book demonstrates powerfully, over and over again, our world is also filled with wonderful stories which demonstrate that authentic Christian faith can be good for people and good for our world.

I am forever indebted to my amazing producer, Kate Cardwell, the source of so many of the ideas and names we present on *Open House*. Her energy is inexhaustible and her doggedness in chasing the best content we can muster never wavers. As we say in the world of journalism, she's a 'gun'!

I am also indebted to publisher David Dixon, editor Owen Salter and designer Joy Lankshear, as well as transcriber Ruth Woellner. Great thanks also to Phillip Randall, CEO of Hope Media, for his ongoing trust and support and Kim Wilkinson for her work on the book, plus the staff of Sydney's Hope 103.2 for their support of *Open House*.

I'm always enormously grateful to my fabulous family for their never-ending support, understanding and love. They are total champions—Meredith, Tristan, Amy, Johanna and Sophie, as well as Susie and Ben.

It's my great hope that this book will both lift our spirits and lift our gaze to a God who, notwithstanding the many failings of those who seek to follow him—me included—always works for our good. Enjoy!

Leigh Hatcher

To Meredith—partner in life, loving mother and grandmother, and 'proofreader in chief'.

openhouse

Lynne McGranger

'Irene Roberts' in *Home and Away*

In the cut-throat world of television drama Lynne McGranger is a stand out. For more than twenty-one years she has played the much-loved character Irene Roberts on the Aussie TV classic *Home and Away*.

She sees her career as a blessing, and many of the cast members regard her as a blessing for the immense impact she has had on the lives of others.

Entwined in her very public life is a very grounded Christian faith. It has given her a deep sense of equilibrium both professionally and personally.

But don't start categorising her as a veteran!

Oh no, I'm a young slip of a thing! I'll let you in on a little secret. A journalist said to me a year ago, 'Do you know that if you're still on the show in a couple of years' time, you're going to be in the *Guinness Book of Records*?' I went, 'Get out of here! Then I'm not going anywhere!'

It's no small achievement. Take us back to when you first auditioned for the role of Irene. Where were you in your life and what did that role mean for you when you got it?
I'd been doing a play in Melbourne and I was asked if I could

audition for a TV mini-series called *Seven Deadly Sins*. I tried out for the 'Envy' episode. When I turned up I was very ill. I had been to my brother-in-law's fortieth birthday and I had food poisoning from dodgy food. Anyway, I struggled through it somehow and I got the job for 'Gluttony', which was a great irony.

About a week or two later my agent in Melbourne rang me about a guest role in *Home and Away*.

So I turned up expecting a 'cattle call', but there was me and Liz Mullinar, the casting agent. I thought, 'This is odd.' Normally you turn up and half the world and his wife's there. A week later I got the phone call that I got the role. The character was a 'thin wasted alcoholic'. Because I was so unwell when I turned up, they'd gone, 'Why don't we ask Lynne McGranger to do that because she looked a shocker!' So that's honestly how I got the role.

The Lord works in mysterious ways.
He certainly does.

Could I ask you a question that I don't think I've ever asked anybody on this program—were you a show-off as a child?
Leigh, I was just about to say, 'Is the Pope a Catholic?', but he is.

That's fine, this is a religious show!
Absolutely, absolutely. I used to put on concerts in the backyard when I was about five or six. I'd make the neighbours pay threepence to come and see me. Yes, I always loved to perform.

You did stand-up comedy at one stage, didn't you?
Yes, when I was pregnant with my daughter! I'd done theatre and I'd done cabaret. I'd put on concerts, done revues at teacher's college, a little bit of telly and short film. So when I was pregnant I thought, 'This stand-up comedy looks like a bit of a lark. I'll give it a try.'

I figured, being pregnant, people wouldn't throw things at me. I was wrong! There would be nights, Leigh, when I would consider myself the funniest human being on the planet. Then there were other nights when I truly just wanted to bury myself in a hole because it was so awful.

I did it for about seven months. I thought it was like jumping out of a plane: I'd done it, I'd survived and I didn't need to do that again. Now that I'd done that, I could do anything!

After playing Irene for twenty-one years, what do you love about her?
What I love about her is that she calls a spade a front-end loader. She is so gutsy and she really takes it up to people. She doesn't really care what others think about her. Of course, she's human too—she loves to be loved. However, if she sees that something is wrong, she'll take it up to somebody, whether it's a fourteen-year-old or Alf Stewart!

Are there things that you don't like about her character?
I'd love her to be a bit more resilient in her faith. She does have a faith, and Irene was given the opportunity to pray publicly when her children were in a terrible situation in a plane crash. The writers wrote that for me.

Lynne, why do you think Home and Away *has been such a success here in Australia and overseas?*
First overseas—particularly in England, Ireland, Wales and Scotland and places like Estonia and Norway and Belgium. I think it's the appeal of the weather and the lifestyle. It's young, there's freedom, fresh air and adventure. There is very much that appeals to overseas people.

As far as Australians go, I just think it's a clever mixture of the writers being able to take thirty or forty set storylines and twist them every so often. On top of that, the producers are savvy enough to be able to go for stationary characters. They seem to love Alf; they seem to love Irene. I am very grateful for that.

Lynne, you've always been very open about your Christian faith. How and where did that start, and what does that mean to you, personally and professionally?

I was churched by my dad in the Anglican Church. I went to Sunday school and was confirmed when I was thirteen. I remember going to a Billy Graham event when I was about thirteen or fourteen. I went down the front and accepted Jesus as my Saviour. I remember it was quite a big moment, but I guess it didn't really compute—it didn't move from my heart to my head.

Over time I definitely did fall away for many, many years, but I always prayed. I always prayed to God. I would pray when I needed him, but I had never really accepted Jesus as my Saviour.

Around the end of 2004 my dad was getting very, very ill with cancer. That was a difficult time because even though he had churched me, and even though I knew he had a fundamental faith, we had never really talked about it. I found it very, very hard—very awkward. I didn't know how to approach Dad.

I remember one day I could feel God working on me and I had prayed about it. It was a Friday and I said, 'Dad, do you think you've booked your seat in heaven?' I didn't know how else to put it. He muttered and mumbled and said, 'You know, I've always believed. I know John 3:16.' I said to him, 'Look, Dad, do you want to talk to somebody—not me, someone who knows what they're talking about? Do you want to talk to the pastor here, or my minister?' He said, 'Yes, I would, but two things—can it be private and can you make it quick?'

On the Sunday I spoke to Ross Hathway, our minister at Kellyville Anglican Church. He said, 'Look, I have the mother of all weeks coming up, but I will move heaven and earth and will pray that I have the time to come down.' I was running late, Ross was running early, so Ross went in to see Dad in private, and as he left he said, 'We had a lovely time. We prayed and we talked about John 3:16. Your father has a surprising amount of biblical knowledge.'

I went in and spoke to Dad and he seemed very much at ease and contented. That was the last time I saw him alive. I still get a bit teary when I talk about it. That had a huge impact on me. I knew without a shadow of a doubt that God had worked through me to reach Dad, to call Dad back.

Among many other things that were going on in my life at the time—relationships, my addiction to smoking and a whole range of things that were going bad in my life—through prayer and through God's constant nudging, I was brought to a point where shortly after Dad's death I asked Jesus into my life as my Saviour.

There have been times when I have done two steps forward, one step back. I don't think there is a Christian on the planet that doesn't do that. That was the absolute zenith of my life where everything came together by God's grace.

And for your dad, eternity was at stake.

Absolutely, and I know without a shadow of a doubt that my father is up there with Jesus and God and that we will see each other again one day. I am eternally thankful to God for taking me on that journey.

Can I ask you, as a performer in television, how does your faith shape your view of yourself? Perhaps a sense of a bigger picture beyond all the pressures and insecurities of your business?

I think in some respects my faith has shaped my view of myself apart from my acting. I have spent so much of my life seeing myself as a reflection of others. My self-worth has often been in how other people see me. It's something that I struggle with still to this very day, even at this ripe old age. By the grace of Jesus I'm learning very slowly that my self-worth should be in God. My self-worth is in the fact that I am a child of God and that Jesus died for me. I am saved by him—I am saved by grace. It doesn't matter diddly-squat what Joe Blow thinks of me.

Because once again eternity is in view.
Yes. You are here one minute and gone the next. We just need to keep our eyes focused above all the time.

How significant has your family been in supporting you and being alongside you through all this?
Oh, unbelievably. Paul, my husband, has been the most amazing support. I could never have done what I've been able to do on *Home and Away* had he not been a 'house-husband' and chief caregiver to our daughter, Clancy. I started all this when she was twenty months old. Of course, now I can't get him back to work! Now he just thinks this is what he does—staying at home and pottering around the garden!

I wouldn't have it any other way. He has been amazing, and Clancy has turned out pretty darn good. I am so thankful to God for that too. She's a great young woman—she's delightful.

And probably following in your footsteps.
Oh yes. I tried to beat it out of her, but, yes, she is at drama school. I just hope and pray she finds great happiness and contentment in her work.

So, Lynne, over twenty-one years you have built up this huge fan base across the country and the world. Have you got a favourite 'fan moment'?
To be honest, Leigh, I have a myriad of great fan moments. I think probably my very favourite was in Ireland. It was our first time in Ireland. We landed in Shannon, picked up a car and Paul was at the wheel screaming at me, 'Where are we going?' I said, 'I don't know—here, you read the map!'

I'm not going to say anything!
We ended up in this pub, walked inside and there were all these 'sea salts', these old salty sea captains with lots of beard and not many teeth and pipes. They really looked like they were in a movie. We walked into the pub, looked up on the TV—and I'm there, on the screen!

It was like being in the Wild West. They hear the door open; they all turn around, look and see me standing there; turn back and look at the television; turn back around and look at me. You could see them gradually pushing their beers away as if to say, 'Oh no, I've really got to stop this drinking!'

And may God strike me down, I was there on the telly as I was standing behind them. It was the most marvellous, surreal encounter. It was lovely, Leigh, and the people of Ireland—and indeed wherever we've been—have been so warm, so friendly and so hospitable.

So after twenty-one years, how much longer will we be seeing you on the telly?
I'm not planning on going anywhere in a hurry. I love my job. My job is just amazing and wonderful. God willing, as long as the show keeps going and as long as people love to watch *Home and Away* at home and abroad, I'd like to think that I'll get carried out of there feet first one day. And then I'll meet my Maker!

Justin Gardner

From 'Underbelly' to church minister

Justin Gardner grew up with the real life characters at the centre of the first *Underbelly* TV series in Melbourne. Most of them are now dead.

Justin was stealing cars at eleven, dealing drugs at twelve and plotting a murder at twenty-two. Incredibly lost and suicidal, he says there was only one place he could turn: to God.

Today he's the senior pastor of the Destiny Centre Christian Church in Victoria and has written about his incredible transformative story in his book *CrimeSon*.

I grew up with them [the *Underbelly* characters] and I used to always hang around amusement joints with them. I was stealing cars with older boys from when I was eleven. Some of those guys were into petty crimes back then, a bit of drugs and different things. As they got older the drugs increased, and wherever there are drugs there are lies, deception and fear—and the rest is history. Most of those guys are dead now.

Justin, when you now look at the Underbelly *TV series and see what happened in their real lives, that was the path you were also on.*
I tried to break away from where those sort of guys were going because they got into heavier drugs. One of the things that saved

my life was a fear of syringes and needles. So when the majority of my friends started using speed and heroin, I didn't. But I was still self-medicating and drinking alcohol and smoking a lot of dope. All that still really messed with my mind.

One interesting term you use to tell your story is being 'dream bankrupt'. What do you mean by that?
I got to the point where I had no dreams left at all. I never had a dream to be married, to have children—the hope of living had completely drained out of me. I was lying on the floor in a place called St Albans and everyone had left me.

Was there no one to whom you could go to cry for help?
No, not at all. No one. I was tormented inside. I was vomiting and shaking every day for a month, maybe more. Inside I was like a raging volcano with suicidal thoughts thousands of times a day. I wasn't sleeping, wasn't eating, and there was no one to help me.

So then at twenty-two you call out to God, but before I ask you about that part of the story, was he ever part of your past?
I was brought up in a Catholic family, so one thing I definitely learnt was that going to church doesn't make you a Christian. Just like going to McDonald's doesn't make you a hamburger! I was brought up in all that, but I never chose Christ for myself.

I saw some hypocrisy in people that started getting to me at a very young age. I'd look at my father—how he was in church and then how he was at home. He was a very violent, very aggressive man and a very hard man to please. He used to put very heavy burdens on me that I could never meet. Because of that there was a lot of frustration and anger in me as a kid that I didn't understand.

I'd also been thieving ever since my hands had been moving. I reckon if you'd asked my mum when I started stealing she would have said, 'Before the womb'.

When I was a teenager, sometimes Christians used to come out onto the streets and tell me about Jesus and tell me how I could be saved. My response to that was I would spit on them and say things about their mums to try and prove that what they were doing wasn't real and that they were fake. But their message eventually won me over in my heart. I never showed them, but years later, when I was suicidal, I knew that I could call out to Christ, as well as to Christians who had been praying for me.

So what happened then when you did that?
Just before I ended up on those floorboards ready to end my life, my mother had invited me to a church in Hoppers Crossing. It was very hard for me to walk in there that night, but I walked up and sat in the front row. I really wanted to sit in the back row, but I was that rebellious I sat in seating reserved for the guest speaker! I didn't realise, but the church people let me know with their body language and their eyes burning into my back. I felt very rejected and left.

Then an old man came outside and shook my hand and apologised. He saw what happened and he said I could sit anywhere I wanted. He was a very genuine man, and his apology touched my heart—even though I didn't accept it and go back in.

Now fast forward to that night on the floor when I'm about to blow my brains out. I called out to Christ and asked him to come into my heart and save me. I still remember it: I said, 'If you just save me and forgive my sins, anything you ask me I'll do it for you. I don't want any of this materialistic stuff anymore, I just want you.' I felt hope come into my heart right there. My suicidal thoughts were still there, but hope had come in and I knew I was right with God.

It was late, maybe one o'clock in the morning, and I thought the first thing I needed to do was ring a church. The first church that came to mind was the one that had just rejected me. So with childlike faith I rang that number and that same old man answered! He was the caretaker at the church. He prayed for me on the phone, set me up to see a pastor the next day and, to cut a long story short, I'm the senior pastor of that church sixteen years later.

Justin, tell me how your life changed after that memorable night.
I meant what I prayed to Jesus, but it was very hard because I'd lived such a dishonest life my whole life. Now I had to learn to be honest. I had to move away from that culture. That was a scary thing.

So I moved to Hoppers Crossing and my mum took me back in, and I started to have my relationship restored with her. I was a broken young man and I was like a baby again. I couldn't read properly or anything like that. My mum would give me my little sister's picture Bible. I'd be in bed at night and she would be praying for me like a child. It was like my childhood that I was robbed of was starting to be restored.

Then I started to renew my own mind and I listened to the Bible on tape. Then I began to read properly and retain what I was reading. I probably listened to up to thirteen sermons a week and read about three books at once for about twelve years straight.

So take us through the journey that then led you to become the senior pastor of that church.
That's a bit of a shock because every time there was a service, I was

there, but I still looked like a drug dealer, covered in gold chains, with a cap and sunglasses. I used to be so embarrassed—week after week I was crying every service. I remember going home and saying to God, 'Why can't I stop crying?' I felt God say to me, 'You'll never cry the same tears twice because I'm healing you from all the pain you've stored up over all those years. If I healed you in one go you wouldn't live through it.'

Then I started serving coffees in church (another form of drug dealing really!). My suicidal thoughts had stopped completely and I've never had them again. I was stirring coffees one day thinking, 'This is the best place I've ever been in my life. I'd be happy to do this for Christ the rest of my life.' I still feel that way today, to tell you the truth.

It was still quite a journey for you, from stirring coffees through all the study required to then become the leader of that church.

I started seeing that even in church culture some people weren't included. So I started reaching out to people who'd never been reached by the church: people in halfway houses, schizophrenics and people battling with alcoholism and drugs. I brought them to church. The senior pastor saw that and he gave me a key one day to the church and said to me, 'Anytime you want to come and open the church and use an office to pray for someone or help someone, here it is.' I can't remember anyone ever trusting me like that before.

So I just started caring for people, bringing people, and before I knew it God told me to go to Bible college. I was in full-time ministry just three years after being saved.

Now I get to minister to millionaires, murderers, homeless people, intellectuals—basically everybody. I know this one thing, that everyone I meet is fighting something. Everyone. I feel sort of equal with them because I'm fighting my own stuff too. Without Christ I'm in big strife.

I have never met a greater love. I never knew that someone could love me more than *I* love me. I never knew that someone could give me underserved grace and mercy and give me a second and a third and endless chances. God doesn't change his mind about me. It is incredible to know that—someone who will never leave me no matter what. And it's not performance based. He's already made up his mind about me. He loves me.

He is a real God and he was a real man—one hundred per cent man, one hundred per cent God who walked this earth. He's still very real now, and he's still very much alive and seated in heaven.

Justin, I think the best way to finish our wonderful conversation is to ask you about your family.

Oh, my family is just incredible. I've got two boys and a beautiful wife. My sister, who was a Christian and who had been praying for me for years, her prayer partner is now my mother-in-law! She was praying for her daughter while my sister was praying for me! I met my wife at a different church and it all clicked. Today I have two sons and my wife is my best friend—it's incredible.

Tell us about those two sons, Davis and Oskar.

When I look over them at night and I see them breathing, I feel nothing but love towards them. I know I'm just an earthly father, but if I can feel that way towards my sons, I can't really grasp the amazing love God feels towards us. When Davis was born, the first time I saw him I felt God say to me, 'This would have been one of the things you would have missed out on if you'd killed yourself all those years ago.' They are just champion kids.

The details of Justin's book, *CrimeSon*, are on his website <www.crimeson.com.au>.

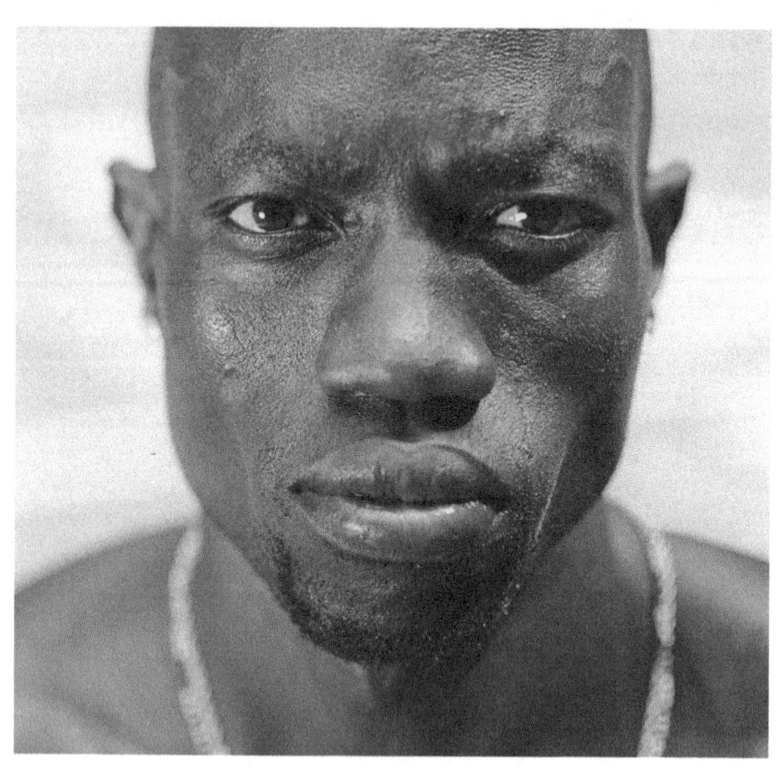

Lopez Lomong

Sudanese refugee, US Olympian

Lopez Lomong was abducted in Southern Sudan at the tender age of six and taken to a rebel army camp to be trained as a child soldier. He and three young friends miraculously escaped through a hole in the fence and ran for three days until they found a refugee camp in Kenya.

Every day for ten years, Lopez ran a 25-kilometre course around the camp. Then at the age of sixteen an opportunity arose after he wrote a letter to a Catholic charity. He was relocated to the USA, where he started a new life and, remarkably, fulfilled a seemingly impossible childhood dream. His story is a modern-day miracle, especially considering that day he was kidnapped from his family.

The only thing I remember was crying, watching my family as I was carried away by guys with guns. They dragged me to a truck covered with a canvas. That truck was so hot and I didn't have shoes. It changed my life completely until today.

Did you ever think you'd see your family again?
No, not at all. I didn't have any sense of where we were going. I just looked back and asked God, 'Why did this happen on Sunday? Why did this happen to me?'

What made you at the age of six cry out to God?
My family are all Christians. The only time we all looked forward to was Sunday, because that was the time when we could sing songs and I'd see my family worshipping. We didn't have an actual building—we just praised God under a tree. We were so happy, but when those people took me away I was so terrified.

They took us away from the truck and blindfolded us. There were about one hundred other kids. Most of us were very hungry and a lot of the kids were actually dying in the process of us being held captive.

So tell us about your escape. How long were you in the camp before you got a chance to make it out through that fence?
Probably about three weeks. We crawled outside and escaped in the middle of the night. The night was so, so dark.

And you ran and ran and ran for days.
We ran and ran three days and three nights. We didn't know what direction we were going, but we had a God who was protecting us. Every time I got so tired and could not go any more, my friends told me, 'You see those hills out there by the horizon? That's where your mum is.' So again I got a huge power coming into me and I'd say, 'OK, let's keep going.'

We got to those hills and then our journey extended to another 30 to 40 kilometres. We kept running and running—we were so very tired. When we slept we would all face the direction where we were going because we didn't want to go back to where we'd come from. We'd wake up in the morning and head off again in that direction. So we just ran and ran until we ended up in a refugee camp.

How did you find that refugee camp?
We ended up being arrested by the border guards between South Sudan and Kenya. By that point I could not walk at all. My feet were bleeding with lots of pus—I was just crawling. I saw the faces of these soldiers on the border and they were different. They weren't that vicious. We realised that we were in the right hands because they were not using their guns or anything. They were protecting us.

They fed us some corn and took us to the Kakuma Refugee Camp, which is not too far from the border. That's where our lives started again—for the next decade.

You have one amazing story in your book, Running for My Life, *about a television hooked up to a car battery that had a tremendous impact on your life.*
In 2000 I was sixteen years old and there was the Sydney Olympics in Australia. We walked about eight kilometres to the house of a Kenyan man. We said to him, 'We'd like to watch the Olympics.' I stood right in front of this little black-and-white TV operated by the car battery, and the first thing that came on was the 400 metres. Michael Johnson was running with 'USA' on his chest.

I saw the whole stadium and this guy run so fast. He beat everybody and then he cried. I was struck by that: 'Why did he cry?' In Africa a grownup must not cry—not even me, a sixteen-year-old. It was amazing to see that and it really opened my mind. I said, 'I would like to run as fast as that guy for that country one day.' That's when my Olympic dream started.

I just started running for my life, inspired by somebody thousands of kilometres away. Deep down it give me the hope that one day I can belong in the Olympics for the United States.

You must have had a tremendous amount of discipline but also energy to run so far—25 kilometres each day.
It was a way of escaping the temptation of eating all the food that was supposed to be rationed for forty-five days. It would be even more than forty-five days before we got another rationing. It was the only thing we could do to distract ourselves from thinking about hunger—we'd go for a run.

And all the time you had this vision of the Olympics still in your mind?
Yes, absolutely, because the moment I saw the Olympic Games in Sydney, I saw another world out there for me. Because running was more like transportation to me; I didn't know that it was a sport. If you want to go from point A to point B and you want to get there quick, you run there. After watching Michael Johnson cry I thought, 'Wow, he wasn't doing this for himself.' It was something bigger. He was running for a purpose.

Now I'm running for God and for people who don't have a chance to tell their story. Today there are kids still in refugee camps, going through what I went through. That's why I'm here to inspire them. I want to tell them that there is more. Think big! You are a son or daughter of God. Somebody is going to come by and pick you up and say, 'Hey, you matter. You go out and practise any sport you want to practise.'

Did you ever think of how you might achieve that dream? How do you go from a Kenyan refugee camp to the Olympics?
It's through God. I prayed every day from the moment I saw that picture on that black-and-white TV. From that moment I started dreaming. Every time I thought about running I also thought, 'One day I will be in the USA—one day.'

With God, blessing takes a while and it takes patience. Even when I came to the United States, although I'd never even won a varsity race, I told my coaches, 'I want to go to the Olympics.' They'd say, 'Oh my goodness, are you serious? How are you going to go to the Olympics when you're still running seventeen minutes for five kilometres?' I always believed God would open the doors.

And you took action after ten years and wrote to a Catholic charity?
After ten years in the refugee camp, the United States government announced it would accept 3500 lost boys. I thought, 'I have to be part of that!' I started writing my story in Swahili, to be translated into English word-by-word. God was there and my name was called. I was just so happy.

So what was it like arriving in the United States for you?
It was amazing. I remember July 31, 2001. My US family had only ever seen this black-and-white, passport-sized photo of me. They put a big sign up saying 'Welcome home'. I'd never had that before. It was just incredible to see. Now I had a childhood again—a childhood and a family that I had never had before.

I was adopted into a new family in Upstate New York. They told me I was going to school. My education level wasn't even like a first-grade education. I'd never owned a pencil, pen, paper or anything in the camp, but now I had my own backpack! I was willing to learn very quickly. I graduated from high school after three years. It was just incredible to have my family there supporting me, cheering me on the whole way.

And still you never lost that vision that you wanted to run and to get to the Olympics?
Oh yeah, I never lost it. I wasn't even an American citizen yet, but

that dream, that power was in my heart the whole time. I had to follow that and keep pursuing it. There is nothing impossible with God—everything is possible. I wanted to give back; I wanted to run for this country.

And then you made the team for 2008?
Yes, yes, I made the team! Even the Olympic trials were hard, but I was just so blessed. I was saying, 'Thank you, God—a lot of people will be watching me and I can really tell my story.' I'm no longer running away for fear of my life, I'm running *toward* something and I'm running for joy, celebrating the gift that God blessed me with. I wanted to multiply it.

When I finished third I called my USA parents and I said, 'You are going to Beijing!' They started crying and said, 'Oh my goodness, you've been saying this since you were sixteen years old!' It is incredible—they ended up coming to the Olympics! To have my family out there and to have people waving the American flag and taking my picture, I thought it was a dream. I started pinching myself to wake up! Once I was a lost boy—nobody even cared for me. But now I am running for the country! I wanted to be a great ambassador and thank the American people for giving me this opportunity.

Lopez, eventually you were re-united with your family in Sudan as well. What was that like?
In 2003 I received a phone call. My mum was actively looking for me after seventeen years of separation. In 2007, after I became an American citizen, we met again. This woman in front of me was my real mother and she started dancing. It just brought tears to my eyes. She was such a strong woman—she never gave up on me.

My dad came over as well and it was just incredible to have a thanksgiving, to sit down at the table and share a meal that we had never shared since I was young. It was such a blessing. It is incredible how God can protect people and eventually reunite them after seventeen years. Isn't it amazing?

Lopez, can I ask you finally: what do you say to God today about the way your life has played out?

I say to God, 'I am your son. You basically rescued me from the wilderness, from all the dangers. I could have been dead somewhere in that camp. But I never give up because you are always there for me.' He is a God of forgiveness. I have already forgiven all the people who kidnapped me because they didn't know what they were doing. I think they were actually doing a good thing for me.

Now is my time to be able to go out and give back with the Lopez Lomong Foundation and give a future to other kids in South Sudan—giving clean water, education, health care and nutrition. I would like to give an opportunity to these kids to get everything that they need. This is the opportunity that the American people gave to me. This is the time for me from South Sudan to tell everybody that we need to get out there and help.

I would also like to offer a shout out to the great Australian government for giving opportunities for a lot of South Sudan refugees. Now we have our opportunity and hope.

You can learn more about Lopez's remarkable story and the Lopez Lomong Foundation at <www.lopezlomong.com>

openhouse
openhouse
openhouse
openhouse

Patricia Weerakoon

Eros, intimacy and the mind of God

Patricia Weerakoon is a fascinating woman who poses this unexpected, arresting question: 'What has God got to do with desire?' Her answer is, 'Lots!'

Patricia explodes the image of Christian people being wowsers, boring or puritanical about sex. She is a medical practitioner turned sexologist. She offers profound insights into the physical, emotional and spiritual dynamics of sex—with a few cheeky observations along the way.

Patricia explained to us how puzzled she always feels that people imagine God to be anti-sex.

People think that the Bible and God are always saying, 'Just don't do it!' They don't realise that the Bible actually says, 'Go ahead and do it! Just do it in a holistic and healthy way and you'll have wonderful fun—great sex!'

Patricia, you completed your medical degree in Sri Lanka, with post-graduate study in Hawaii. What drew you to sex?
I was one of the few females on the faculty so I was asked to teach sex and reproduction. When I went to Hawaii I also worked with

a sexologist in sexual health clinics, and I realised then that sex was actually so beautiful. Our bodies are created for wonderful sex, and our sexual responses are so beautifully matched as male and female. So there was the beauty and the purity. But then on the other side there was this power and hunger of sex. People longed to have good sex but looked in all the wrong places.

As a Christian, I really had to look at that and think, 'How does this fit in with what God has been telling us—his created and spoken pattern for good sex?'

You've also looked into brain chemistry and found some really interesting things about the three stages of sex through our lives.
This is fairly recent work coming from the laboratories of Professor Helen Fisher and her group. They have worked with magnetic resonance imaging and allowed us to look into the brain and see which bits light up when things happen.

What we're finding is that there are three consequential stages. First, there is sexual desire, which is like an appetite. It starts in your early teens and then it's this bubbling cauldron of desire for sex. Then all this energy is focused onto one person when you fall in love. That's known as the limerence phase. There are chemicals like dopamine and endorphins which give you the euphoria and excitement when that person takes over and inhabits your brain. Finally, you go into an attachment phase, which is driven by other chemicals that we call the 'cuddle hormones'.

How long do each of those phases typically last?
Desire is actually a lifelong thing. Desire is just an appetite that says, 'I want sex.'

Falling in love, that crazy hot stage of love, fortunately doesn't last for more than twelve to eighteen months. I've been married thirty-eight years, and if I started palpitating every time I saw my husband, I wouldn't be alive right now!

Then when you find 'the one' and you get married and have sex, you move into that cuddle phase. That lasts a lifetime.

Does casual sex fit into that at all?

It does not. When you have sex with someone, you bond. You think you are in love, you have sex and you form a mini-bond. Then when you move on, you tear yourself apart.

Every time you have sex, of course, it feels great because that is the way we're created. We are created to enjoy that experience. It was meant to be wonderful. Just imagine when God said, 'Go out and procreate and fill the world'—what if he made it the most boring thing in the world to do? What if it was like doing your tax return or taking the garbage out? Who would do it? We wouldn't have a population! We are created to procreate. It's a wonderful thing that God made it recreational to procreate.

But you also say that God makes it for fidelity.

Of course, because the more you are with a person and the more sex you have, the more you bond. Sexual intercourse is the most intimate and trusting thing you will ever do with another human being. It's an act of absolute intimacy. At that point you form a 'one flesh' bond, and that is meant to remain and build together as one man and one woman for life.

Can I ask you about one very powerful modern dynamic in our society—pornography. What do you say about that?

Pornography is now a $70 billion-plus industry globally. The average age at which children first view pornography is eleven to thirteen years. The research today tells us that almost every young man at some time has viewed porn.

Every pornographic image and every video that feeds into the brain is rewiring the brain circuits. It's physically building connections. Those connections that are used over and over again are kept. I tell teenagers that the Bible speaks of feeding your mind on pure and good things, and that actually means something when you're young.

Adult brains are also rewired by porn to desire porn. That's why as a therapist I see porn use destroying many relationships—including Christian relationships.

Are you able to rewire brains back to a better state?
Yes, but it takes time. It takes a lot of grace—and I am using that word very deliberately because it needs forgiveness and it needs repentance. It needs that ability to stay together as a couple and rebuild the images and the wiring.

So you say God's plan is for good sex. How do you come to that conclusion?
Oh, the whole Bible is so sex positive! It's one of the most sex positive or sexiest books I've ever read—and I've read some in my time!

It starts with sex. Adam and Eve in the garden—for goodness' sake, they were perfect! Adam with the perfect six-pack and so well adorned he probably needed a whole lot of fig leaves! Eve was just perfect, no boob jobs or Botox. Then we look at the book of Revelation and we see Christ coming back to claim his church—what a wedding, what a honeymoon, what a consummation that's going to be! And then we have the sealed section right in the middle, the Song of Songs—what erotic poetry! How can all that not be about love?

So I'm sure you would be surprised at the image of the Christian person being anti-sex or negatively hung up about sex.

A very good friend of mine, a professor in America, said to me, 'Patricia, how is it even possible that you are a sexologist and a Christian? Christians are trying to close us all down and get rid of us.' I said, 'I have the privilege of having a personal relationship with the Creator of sex.'

God created us male and female, and our genitals fit so perfectly. It's like an engineering marvel. I am an anatomist and physiologist, and I just cannot get over the beauty of it all. God wants the best for us.

But, of course, as a fallen people we mess it up. That's why we have to go back to God's pattern and redeem sex. We have not given young people the message that love is not necessarily about 'making love' alone.

So you've painted that picture of the spunky Adam and Eve at the dawn of creation. The reality is, though, that those six packs start to fade. How do we remain attached and vibrant in our sex life despite the onslaught of the years?

I just love this because it again takes us back to fairly new research. They've looked into the brains of adults who have been married for some time who said that they were happily married and had reasonably good sex. They found the parts of the brain that are involved in love still light up—but not in that crazy way. It's a modulated light up, a nice steady light that old eyes can take.

This is also really good for your children to be aware of. A lot of young people say, 'We would love to know about our parent's love stories and learn about sex from them.' Parents are not sharing their values with their children. So this is also a call to Christian parents, and even to grandparents, to talk to children about their love stories. They will revitalise *their* love, and they will also be teaching their children what good love is—the values of family, a man and woman, husband and wife.

Now, doctor, you said I can ask you anything?
Anything!

OK, here it comes. Thirty-eight years of marriage—how's the sex life?
My husband has always known that he was marrying this crazy sexologist woman! We are both Christians. We were friends and mates before we ever slept together after marriage.

My husband has this ability to keep me grounded. I would have done the craziest, sexiest things during the day, and when we are together in the evening we have our together time; but we must also have our God time. So he grounds me and brings us back to that primary identity, that firstly we are man and woman as Christians before Christ. Then all the fun and fluff and sex are added to that!

So what would you say is the key to a good sex life and a good marriage?
First, keep a focus on what really matters in your relationship. If I am talking to Christian couples, I will say to remember that this is a partnership. It's not about getting *your* desires met, but about caring for the other person and wanting what is best for them.

It's a bit like Christ-like love. Christ cared so much for us he went to the cross. My husband cares so much for me that he would die for me. So I am willing to give anything and obey what he wants me to do. In a tiny way our marriages do exemplify Christ and the church.

If we can keep that in our minds and show that to our children and the world, they will look at us and say, 'I want a piece of what they have.'

Mark Scott

ABC Managing Director

My conversation with Mark Scott ranged across all three of the *Open House* benchmarks—life, faith and culture. For the last seven years he has headed up arguably the most significant cultural organisation in Australia. It reaches into seventy-five per cent of homes and claims a public approval rating of ninety per cent.

His life and his way of working have been shaped by an authentic Christian faith (without being a 'Bible basher'!). He took on this very demanding, high profile job at the age of forty-three. At the time it was a daunting prospect.

I remember being terribly surprised when I got the job. I said to people at the time that the only thing I really knew about broadcasting was how to turn on the set! I'd never worked in radio. I'd never worked in television. I'd worked in newspapers and I was comfortable around a media environment, but it was a great honour and very daunting. The ABC had been through controversial times and I felt it was going to be a big stretch. I think the Board took a punt on me, being quite young and inexperienced.

You also took it on at a particularly critical time in media, when the rush of change we're drowning in at the moment was just starting. Twitter was starting and YouTube was just a year old. How did you come to grips with what you could do or should do at the ABC?

I think a few things were helpful to me. The first was coming from the newspaper experience [as editorial director at Fairfax]. Newspapers had already seen so much change. I think I'd seen enough of newspapers to know that to be too conservative and too defensive was a problematic path.

The other thing I could see at the ABC was this enormous potential. When I went there I remember people saying to me, 'Oh, you're going to find it a very broken place. Very negative, very cynical—they've had some tough times.' Actually, when I arrived and spent some time talking to people, I thought it was in better shape than anybody had told me. I thought it was in better shape than the ABC had told itself.

In this era of media convergence, where you want to have television and radio, online and mobile, the ABC had all that. The ABC was already a very complete new-age media organisation. It just needed to organise itself in a way that took advantage of those attributes. That's what we started to do.

You then went on to lead a significant breakthrough into digital media and social media that demanded a great deal of change and a great deal of new thinking and hard work. How did you pull all this off without mass walk-outs?

There is a line I like from the novel *The Leopard* which says, 'If we want things to stay the way they are, everything will have to change.'

I spent a lot of time talking with the ABC staff about their love of the ABC and their understanding of the important role the ABC had played in Australian life. We talked a lot about wanting the ABC to be as loved and respected for our children's generation and our grandchildren's generation as it was for us and our parents and our grandparents. To play that role we needed to recognise it would have to change. Standing still and just doing what we had always done—being that great nostalgic broadcaster—wasn't going to guarantee its future. So it was quite important to get people on board and say, 'The future is coming; are we going to be part of it or not?'

I also thought we had the best people in the Australian media, and once they put their mind to it they did extraordinary things. One of the stories I like is the ABC's creation of *iview*. I had heard that the BBC was creating this 'catch up' television service. They had spent £100 million on it. I pulled our team together and said, 'We need one of these things, but we have no budget at all—off you go!' And they did! Innovation loves constraints, and they found a way to create things through their own energy and ingenuity. Today *iview* is a terrific service.

I'd like you to take us through your twin journeys of Christian faith and journalism. First your faith—can you speak about how it's shaped who you are?

I came from a Christian home and reached a personal point of decision myself. That was an important shaper of who I was at school and also at university. I made great Christian friends at university and they still form our core friendships today. That's where I met my wife Briony, and she's a woman of faith. We married young and we grew up together.

I think to me Christianity really *is* a journey. I feel like I'm constantly coming up with more questions than answers. There's a lot I don't know. But I really feel that as you live the Christian life, as you become and try to be a follower of Jesus, those questions get answered as you go down the road. That's the way it has been with me.

So it's who I am. I'm indivisible from it, and I think it's shaped how I view the world and how I work with people, and hopefully the person I am.

So how would you say it influences or informs how you work in a job like yours—and especially, in such a people business, how you relate to people?

I'm almost happy for others to make a judgment of that rather than me. I just hope that the people who work closely with me aren't surprised to discover that I'm a Christian and don't feel that's massively inconceivable, given the person I am around the office!

I think that you do get opportunities, particularly as a leader, to be able to demonstrate the value of every person—that every person has a story, that every person is on a journey. To create an environment where those values are important and that allows everyone to do their best work. And I think it applies to every organisation. Briony runs a school, and we often talk about how these are really people-focused, people-centred organisations. I think as you put the people first, a lot of the other good things come on the back of that.

Can you take us through your journalism journey? It was ignited, I believe, in one defining moment at the Smithsonian Institution in the US at the age of seventeen.

The Smithsonian Museum is a great museum in Washington. I remember standing there and it was the first time I'd ever seen a news tickertape. This machine was spitting out all the news from around the world. I'd never seen that before, and I remember being mesmerised by the fact that news was happening everywhere and this was the first place you would read it.

Much later, when I became a journalist and I was an editor at the *[Sydney Morning] Herald*, I would sit at a computer and you'd see all the news coming in from around the world. One of the great things about Twitter is that now anybody can sign up to follow CNN, the ABC, *The New York Times*, the world's news services, and everybody is now plugged into the immediacy and energy that is a dynamic news environment.

So I always loved news as a kid. I read newspapers and TIME Magazine and watched the news—I always wanted to work in news and journalism. I still think newsrooms are the single most interesting place to be. They are full of vibrant characters, full of people who know what is going on. They are great, great personalities.

Do you ever pinch yourself and wonder, considering where you come from and where you are now, 'How did I get here?'
Absolutely. It's one of the reasons I don't believe in reincarnation, because the next time round it would never be as good as this time! I got the million-to-one shot first up. I'm constantly astounded at the opportunities that have opened up for me. It's been a great blessing.

So you've led this incredible transformation over the last seven years. I'm keen to ask where you think it is going to move in the next seven.
There is a law on technological change which I quite like. It says, 'The impact of technological change is often overestimated in the short-term but underestimated in the long-term.'

I think we're really just beginning to scratch the surface of what it will mean for fast broadband to be everywhere, for everyone to be instantly connected no matter where they are. I expect you'll have full streaming of television networks to everyone's phone and everyone's tablet. The media experience will be absolutely portable and immediately available everywhere.

I think we'll see far more content created by our audience and seamlessly put into the content that we are creating. So it will be almost like a public/private partnership or a professional/amateur partnership around news creation. I think we will experience content immediately from anywhere around the world. Australians will no longer wait for the movie or television show to arrive from the States. As it's broadcast in one place it will be broadcast every place.

That also means that if you're a broadcaster or a filmmaker here you'll be facing global competition. You will really need to know what it is you are offering that is distinctive and rare and unique, because unless you are distinctive or rare or unique, you are going to really struggle to cut through and compete in this global media era.

Can we wrap up with a personal look at yours and Briony's life? I've often seen you from afar and thought, 'Oh, there's a power couple!' She heads up Wenona, the private girls' school.
She's very powerful!

Yes, and so are you! So how do you find space in your head or your life for each other and for your three daughters?
I think one of the things we've noticed over the years is that we are a pretty tight pack of five. Our friends are very tolerant at times that

we're busy and sometimes hard to track down. However, we have always kept time for each other and that's been a priority.

As I said earlier, Briony and I married quite young and we've really grown up together. I think we keep ourselves very grounded and very centred. We talk often through the day and share our stories. We don't live our lives in isolation from each other and don't live our lives in isolation from the family.

One of the great things about the kids is they keep you very grounded and don't take you the least bit seriously. They mock us constantly and I find that quite useful!

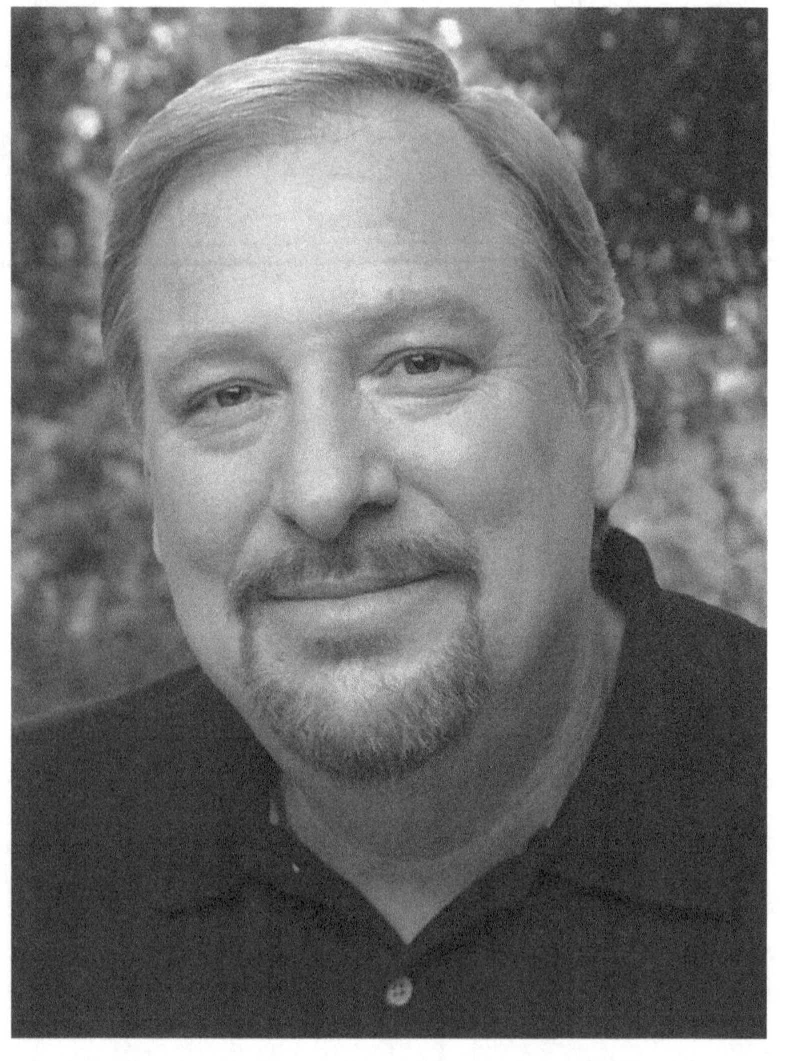

Rick Warren

AUTHOR OF *THE PURPOSE DRIVEN LIFE*

In 2005 TIME Magazine listed Rick Warren among the one hundred most influential people in the world. Now he's among the top twenty most influential individuals on Twitter, with three-quarters of a million followers. He pastors America's biggest church, Saddleback Church in California, and a decade ago wrote *The Purpose Driven Life*, which has now sold thirty-two million copies in fifty languages around the world.

Rick joined us on *Open House* to mark the tenth anniversary of the book, which has been retooled and re-released with two significant new chapters.

For all his notoriety and achievements, Rick Warren humbly, sincerely applies one of the key themes of *The Purpose Driven Life* to himself, many times a day: that 'it's not about you'. So how was it that he came to write the book in the first place?

Leigh, I think there are three fundamental questions of life that everybody has to deal with, regardless of age, race or even faith. The first is the question of existence: 'Why am I alive?' The second is the question of intention: 'Does my life have a purpose?' The third is the question of significance: 'Does my life matter?'

These are so universal that I thought I needed to study what God has to say about them. The book actually took me about twenty years to write because I was thinking through this for nearly twenty years. When I started writing, it took me seven months to get it all down.

My standard day was this: I would get up at about 4.30 in the morning and I wouldn't shave or shower or eat. I would go to a little study and arrive there about five o'clock, and I would just keep typing on a computer until about noon. By then I would feel a little antsy and my ADD would kick in. So I had to get with some people. One of my staffers would come and I'd eat lunch with them, walk around a little bit, shower and shave and go back to writing at one o'clock. I'd type until about five, then go home, eat dinner, play with the kids and get into bed by about eight o'clock. I did that for seven months.

During that time I never knew that the book was going to be a bestseller. But I did know that it was anointed. Many times as I was writing it, tears would be flowing down my face. I would be reading what I was writing and think, 'I'm not this good; I don't think this way.' I knew that I was being guided, that I was being led by the Spirit. Many times I would write something and I would think, '*I* need this; this is for me; this is what I need to hear.' I had many holy moments over those seven months of writing.

Rick, as the impact of the book became evident in the early days just after its release, what was your response?

My first response to the success of the book was, 'Why me?' I'm not even a professional writer. I'm simply a pastor. The biggest surprise is that I got to write the book. Later I came to believe that God allowed me to write the book because he knew what I would do as a result of it.

We used all of the money that the book brought in, all of the income, to start an international program called 'The PEACE Plan'. P is for 'Plant churches that promote reconciliation'; E is 'Equip servant leaders'; A is 'Assist the poor'; C is 'Care for the sick'; and E is 'Educate the next generation'. These are five things that Jesus did in his ministry, and they attack five giant problems in the world. I'm happy to say the PEACE Plan is now being done in all 196 nations of the world. So the book ended up funding a major ministry that has probably blessed even more people now than the book.

So now to mark ten years of The Purpose Driven Life, *there is this retooled, re-released version with the addition of two chapters—'The Envy Trap' and 'The People Pleaser Trap'—based on the enormous feedback you received.*

I define envy as 'I must be *like* you to be happy' and people pleasing as 'I must be *liked by* you to be happy'. I believe these are the two greatest barriers to fulfilling your life purpose.

If you worry about what other people think, you are never going to fulfil God's purpose for your life. I talk to many people who say, 'I know what I am called to do, I know what my purpose is, but I'm afraid that my husband, or my wife, or my boyfriend, or my parents won't approve.' If we fear the disapproval of other people, it can keep us from fulfilling our purpose in life in a major way.

Envy is the other barrier. When I'm trying to be like other people, I can't be who God made me to be.

So what is your overarching solution or way forward from those two traps—envy and people pleasing?
It goes back to the first chapter and the first sentence of the book: 'It's not about you.' The title of that first chapter is 'It All Starts with God'. If I focus on God then I'm going to live for what I call 'an audience of one' and I'm not worried about what other people think. I know that if I please God it doesn't matter whether I please anybody else, and if I please God it will always be the right thing.

Rick, of the all the responses that you mentioned to the book, could I get you to recount one in particular for us—that of a hostage situation in 2005?
Yes. In Atlanta there was a criminal named Brian Nichols who was taken to court to be sentenced. While he was in court, this criminal grabbed the gun of the guard who was guarding the judge in the courtroom and shot and killed four people and escaped.

There was a massive manhunt across the city of Atlanta to find Brian Nichols over an entire weekend. One night he broke into a house and took a young woman named Ashley Smith hostage. He tied her up and put her in the bathtub. Ashley Smith was at that time a drug addict trying to break a habit. She had also been going to a church and had been given *The Purpose Driven Life*, which she was reading. It was changing her life. She was actually reading it when Brian Nichols tied her up, and he began to talk about it with her. She said, 'You know, God has a purpose for your life. I've been reading about it in this book.' He said, 'Really?' She said, 'Can I read it to you?' So she read *The Purpose Driven Life* to this man who was her captor. She convinced him to set her free and turn himself in to the police—all because he read the book.

Rick, can I take you back much further to one particular moment in your life, when you were a nineteen-year-old Bible student and you and a friend drove about 500 kilometres to hear one particular speaker.
I was going to a Baptist college and that day Dr W.A. Criswell, who was the pastor for fifty years of the First Baptist Church of Dallas, was speaking in Northern California. I had always been amazed by this man who spent fifty years in one church. It was the largest church in America at that time, and Dr Criswell was the most respected pastor in America at that time. My friend and I played hooky and drove to Northern California to hear this man of God preach.

While I was there, I heard him tell the story of how he'd made a commitment to spend his entire life pastoring one church, and so I made that same commitment that day. 'Lord, give me the privilege of spending my entire life in one church.'

After the service I went up to meet him, just to shake hands with this spiritual giant. As I walked up to him he looked at me with very kind eyes and he said, 'Young man, I feel led to pray for you.' So he put his hands on my head and he began to pray, and he said, 'Lord, I ask you to bless this young man, and may his church grow to twice the size of Dallas.' By now tears were falling down my eyes.

Little did I know that that actually would be like a prophecy that would come true, because today Saddleback is more than twice that size, with about one hundred thousand names on our roll of attenders. We have about twenty thousand people who come to the service every weekend. We have about six thousand small groups that meet in Bible study and about thirty-two thousand people in those Bible studies. We are the only church in America, Leigh, that has more people in Bible study in small groups than it has on the weekend.

When we started the PEACE Plan over ten years ago, we set as our goal that by 2010 we would be the first church in history to have sent our members on mission to every nation in the world—all 196 of them. Over the next ten years we sent out 14,869 Saddleback members to go plant churches, equip leaders, assist the poor, care for the sick and educate the next generation in every nation; and on November 18, 2010, we went to nation 196, a little island in the Caribbean called St Kitts. Now, for our next decade, we're going after what we call the 'unreached tribes'—there are 3600 'unengaged' tribes which have no church, no Bible, no Christians. We want to help raise up churches around the world to make sure that, by the end of this decade, there is a Bible and a church in every one of those tribes.

Rick, with everything that has, under God, happened around you, how have you kept your head through it all?

It is by constantly repeating the first sentence of the book. When I wrote that first sentence, 'It's not about you', I honestly didn't know how many times my own life would be tested by that statement.

Since the book came out ten years ago, I've had to say that to myself, quietly as a prayer, sometimes five or ten times a day. So when I'm criticised I say, 'It's not about you.' And when I'm praised I say, 'It's not about you.' And when things get tough and we have the inevitable difficulties and delays and dead-ends, I say, 'It's not about you.' When we have defeats I say, 'It's not about you', and when we have victories I say, 'It's not about you.' It's all about God. I didn't know that I was going to be tested on that statement every day for the rest of my life.

That's the key: to walk humbly before the Lord in dependence. Humility is not denying your strengths; humility is being honest about your weaknesses. The more honest you are about your weaknesses, the more authentic you are. The more humble you are, the more of God's grace you get; and the more of God's grace you get, the more power you have.

Rick, back in 2005 TIME Magazine judged you to be among the top one hundred most influential people in the world. How do you desire to use that influence?

When I began to get more notoriety because of the book, I had to begin to pray about what I call 'the stewardship of affluence' and 'the stewardship of influence'. The easier part was to deal with the money. We just gave it all away. My wife and I are reverse tithers, which means we actually give away ninety-one per cent of our income and we live on nine per cent.

The hard part was that 'stewardship of influence'. I don't think God gives you influence or power just so you can be famous, or so you can be prideful or arrogant. In Psalm 72, which is Solomon's prayer for influence, the Bible teaches us that the purpose of influence is to speak up for those who have no influence. So I committed to use whatever affluence or whatever influence God had given me to help people who have no influence.

That's how I've used it. It is not for our benefit—'it's not about you'—it's to be used for people with no influence. So we speak up. We have ministries to orphans because they have no influence. We have ministries to the sick because they have very little influence. We have ministries to the poor because they have very little influence. If you follow the ministry of Jesus you will use your influence to help those who don't have it.

To learn more about the PEACE Plan visit <www.thepeaceplan.com>.

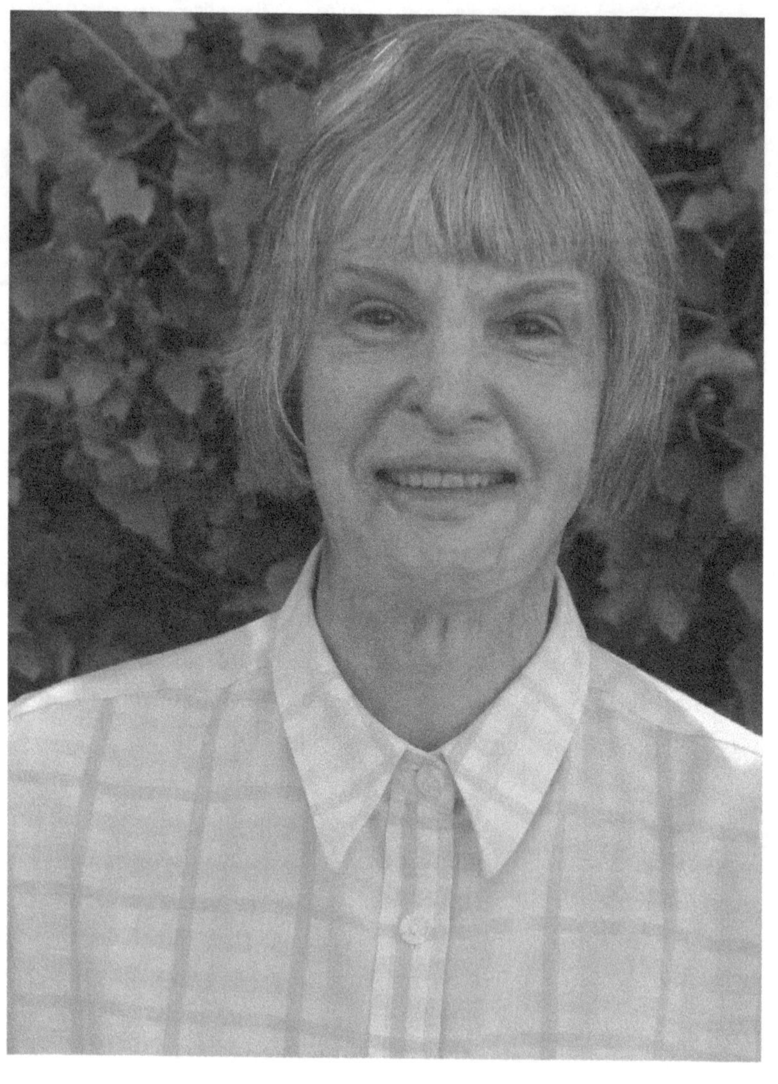

Ann Fogarty

Ash Wednesday bushfire survivor

On February 16, 1983 the Ash Wednesday bushfires in Victoria and South Australia claimed the lives of seventy-five people. Some 2600 were injured. The enormous trials, turmoil and tragedy of that day are in many ways embodied in the life of Ann Fogarty. Her life was profoundly changed forever.

It's a miracle that she even survived, with burns to eighty-five per cent of her body. Seventy per cent of those were third degree. Doctors, nurses, family and friends expected her to die.

More than thirty years on, the scars remain. But Ann has opened up about her remarkable fight for life in a book called *Forged with Flames*, which won the 2013 Australian Christian Book of the Year award. She says her story doesn't have a fairy-tale ending, but it does have hope.

The legacy of it all keeps revealing itself, year after year. At first it was just a physical recovery, and once I'd recovered physically, I thought I would go on to live a normal life. It was also a recovery of my faith, which I didn't lose but had to re-establish in a different way. It has affected me emotionally and mentally. I've suffered from post-traumatic stress, which continues—I can sometimes be totally paralysed by anxiety. I am left with physical difficulties—for instance, I can't keep my body temperature stable. So there is this life-long legacy, which I'm glad I didn't know about at the beginning.

I would love my old body back, particularly my face. But I do look at my body quite differently now and that's been marvellous. I've developed a real respect and admiration for my body, and that's made me look at my scars differently.

Ann, in your book you say that everything felt so perfect in your life just before those terrible fires.
Yes. We had had a wonderful Christmas with family and close friends. I had two little daughters aged six and four and we were just so happy. I don't know that I've ever been in a happier place. It's good that none of us knew what was looming ahead.

Can I take you to that day when the fires hit your town. Did you have any inkling about how severe they would be?
I didn't. I'd grown up in England where you just never heard of a bushfire. I knew in the morning it was extraordinarily hot. That's what I remember as I said good bye to my husband and took my girls to school and kindergarten.

I lived then in a little community called Upper Beaconsfield in Victoria and it was your typical lovely bush town. It was full of beautiful trees and birds and wildlife. Coming from England, that was just enchanting. It felt like a wonderful place to bring up two little girls.

On that day I just did what I normally did, picked up the girls from school. At about 4.45 pm I was looking out of the kitchen window, which overlooked all the bush beyond, and I saw plumes of smoke coming up behind the trees. I had a pang of fear then that this just wasn't right. It looked awfully close.

At about 8.45 that night an emergency vehicle came up the road and someone was yelling, 'Get out now! The wind is about to change!' So I dashed inside and got my two girls and our two dogs and we went and got into the neighbour's car. Before we could set off we realised that one of their children was missing, so we all jumped out. But by the time we realised we couldn't find him, it was too late to escape. The trees were on fire at the top and the wind was howling with an intensity I've never experienced. So we knew we had to shelter. My neighbours had an above ground pool, so we just rushed down there, jumped in and wet all the children.

Then my neighbour, Carol, went up to the house and got two blankets, which we wet. Because branches that were on fire were already falling into the pool, we thought we'd shelter beside it. There was no vegetation, just rocks at one side, so we thought this was a really safe place to be. However, there were fireballs flying ahead of the main fire front and amazingly, unluckily, one of them found this little narrow passage between the rocks and the pool. Because I was beside the pool, they hit me and that's when my injuries happened.

Ann, can I ask you to describe two things for us: the sound of that moment and the fear that you felt as the flames were heading towards you?

Well, the sound was like something I have never heard. One thousand express trains comes a little bit close to it. It was just such a roar. I'd never heard anything before or since like it. You knew that something ominous was happening. And the fear I was feeling: I have to be honest and say I have never been as afraid as I was in that moment. It just eclipsed all my other fears, and I was very familiar with fear.

And the pain, Ann?
The pain also was indescribable. I remember just screaming out, 'Oh God, please let me die.' That was the only way I felt I could escape this terrible, excruciating pain.

So what happened after the fireball swept through?
My neighbour, Alan, who'd been protecting the house, heard me scream and came down, and wonderful Allen lifted me up and put me in the pool, burning his arms and hands in the process. He definitely saved my life at that point. Carol's twelve-year-old daughter, Janet, was also looking after me, and every time flames came near she'd push me under the water to keep me safe. It was a remarkable thing for a little girl to do.

I was in the pool for what felt like hours, but I've been told it was fifteen minutes. At the end of that fifteen minutes I just knew my legs couldn't hold me up any more. I had a fresh pang of fear because I thought I was going to have to sit down and I'd drown. I couldn't keep my head above the water.

At that very moment, a fireman arrived. It was as if at every point there was someone there, just when I was on the brink of death. He lifted me out and took me to the fire truck where my girls were. Someone popped me in the back of a police car and took me down to the refuge centre.

And then to the hospital, where your life was hanging by a thread and the nurses and the doctors were quite pessimistic about your condition.
Yes, they were. They'd never had anyone survive with that covering of third-degree burns.

Did you feel like giving up?
I'm sure I did. I don't remember feeling like giving up because I was terrified of dying. I think that fear kept me alive.

There were also a few glimmers of hope during your long hospital stay.
There were. The most amazing magical thing happened. I loved to play the flute, and my hero was James Galway, the great flautist. He was out here in Australia at the end of May and we had tickets to go and hear him, but there was no way I could make it. I couldn't even get out of bed or do anything. Then one day he walked into my room with his golden flute and his tin whistles and he played for me for an hour!

What that did to me was remind me how amazing life can be in the middle of a nightmare. That was something I will never, ever forget, and it encouraged me beyond words. I still get a glow of warmth every time I think of it.

That wasn't all though—there was a letter from Cliff Richard.
There was, yes—my other hero! 'With lots of love, Ann, and get well soon', and kisses. That was just remarkable.

There were clearly lots of people in your corner and behind you in this.
There were. I didn't realise this until afterwards. I belonged to our local church and was very close to a lot of people there. They'd organised a prayer chain all around the world—people were praying for me night and day. I remember one of my friends saying, 'We just prayed for you for twenty-four hours and I had the two-to-four o'clock slot in the morning.' I thought, 'Wow, how wonderful that people are getting up at that time and praying for me.' It was all inexpressibly wonderful.

Ann, how long were you on the critical list before you started to emerge into something of a normal life?
I was almost three months in intensive care. I could have died, I guess, at any time, so that was the most critical period. Then I went back to the burns unit for a further two-and-a-bit months, and then for the rest of the year I went to a rehab hospital. I came home the day before Christmas, which was wonderful.

It wasn't until six months after the fire that you were able to hold your daughter again, was it?
My two daughters were only six and four. My eldest daughter, Sarah, had said, 'That doesn't look like my mum', and she now says the only thing she recognised about me were my eyes. My youngest, Rachel, just said, 'That's not my mum' and wouldn't come into the ward. One day Terry, my husband, just picked her up and brought her in kicking and screaming because she wouldn't come anywhere near me. She only agreed to be in the room because I had a drawer full of lollies! It was sheer bribery to get her in, but she did not want me to touch her.

It made me feel like I'd lost the girls. I went through a period of thinking they must have died because I hadn't seen them. I hadn't seen my face at that stage and I couldn't imagine how I must have looked, that my own daughters didn't even recognise me. That was very distressing.

Can I ask you to take us to that moment when you first saw your face again?
That was about five months after the fires. One evening I was lying in bed and I just knew that I had to see what I looked like. So I asked the nurse on duty if she'd bring me a mirror. She was very

reluctant, and that made me a little bit suspicious. She eventually brought one in, and in that moment I understood why the girls hadn't recognised me. It certainly wasn't me looking back, and I just kept saying to the nurse through my tears, 'But I'm so ugly.' That was the thing that really hit me: the ugliness of my face.

How long did it take for you to work through that?
It took me twenty years, really, to work through that. For twenty years I wished for a different face.

I had a lot of reaction from other people. I know children are just honest and up front, but one day a young boy looked at me and said, 'Yuk!' And that's how I felt about myself. It seemed to me a confirmation of how other people were seeing me.

But then twenty years on I suddenly had this amazing realisation that my body was extraordinary. It had carried me through thick and thin—my heart kept beating and I could walk anywhere that I wanted to go within reason.

Where did that change of framework come from?
It came because I had breast cancer. I had to have a mastectomy, which I was so angry about. One day I was at my GP's and he was taking my blood pressure. He simply said, 'It's normal.' Suddenly I had this moment of, 'Wow! This body!' In that moment I did a 360° turn. I had so much respect and love for my body. It altered all my feelings about my scars and about myself.

Ann, you spoke earlier about the great challenge, understandably, that this presented to your Christian faith. How did you work through this before God?
I was so sure on the night of the fire as we sheltered. I remember

saying to the others, 'Don't worry, God will keep us safe.' Then to find that I, who had the deep belief, ended up with such terrible injuries . . . it made me feel abandoned. I felt my whole idea of God had come crashing down. I felt let down, disappointed. And, yes, it took me a long time, before God, to work that out.

However, I couldn't deny his presence; it was everywhere. In Allen, who'd save my life; in Tony, the fireman who'd appeared at the right time; in the nurses and doctors. I also had an angel sitting in my room the whole time in intensive care. I saw her and I knew it wasn't a hallucination. So on the one hand my whole belief and trust in God had been shattered, but in another way his presence was so real that I couldn't really let go. It was undeniable.

There was my wonderful minister, Roger. He always made the time to come in and talk to me about God. In many ways other people did the believing for me. I remember one good friend, who used to come in every day, said to me, 'You have to let others do the believing for you now.'

The most wonderful thing I found out about God was when I finally came home and was able to express some of my anger and disappointment. He said to me, 'I can take it—just spill it out as often as you like.' Eventually that was very, very healing.

I'm sure that you'd probably never have gained so many of these insights without this terrible tragedy.

No. I did have a deep faith, but it wasn't a really relational faith like it is now. I feel God is my best friend, my rock. I don't do anything without talking to him first. So I've moved into a totally different relationship with him, one where I don't actually have to understand everything and I can be real. I know he loves me and I love him. It's all very, very precious now.

So you're able to end your book by saying, 'This story doesn't end in a fairy tale but it does have hope.'
Yes. Life is still wonderful—to be alive! Life can take you to extraordinarily painful places, but it can also take you to extraordinarily amazing places.

You can find details of Ann's book, *Forged with Flames*, published by Wild Dingo Press, at <www.wilddingopress.com.au/Books/Forged-with-Flames>.

Baroness Caroline Cox

Member of the House of Lords, founder of HART

One UK commentator wrote this about Baroness Caroline Cox: 'If there is an ignored conflict in the world, particularly one in which Christians are facing persecution, you can bet this seventy-year-old will be there.'

Baroness Cox was made a life peer in the British House of Lords thirty years ago and is one of its former Deputy Speakers. A champion of human rights, she has also been described as 'a British Joan of Arc for our times'. For instance, she undertook numbers of trips to Sudan during which she rescued more than two thousand slaves by paying around $200,000 raised by Christian church groups.

She was in Australia promoting the work of HART—the Humanitarian Aid Relief Trust—which she founded. For all of her daring, barnstorming work, she also knows what it is to be afraid.

When I go into one of those conflict zones, I shrink and get what I call my 'fit of faithless, fearful dread'—and I don't really want to go. I remember once I had a fit of that dread on a Saturday afternoon, but when I went to church the next morning, the gospel reading was this: 'He who does leave husband, wife, brothers and sisters for my sake will find new brothers and sisters, even under persecution.' It is so true. When you do go beyond your frontier of fear to those frontlines of faith and freedom, you meet the most wonderful people. You come back receiving more than you can ever, ever give.

So clearly it has been that faith that has driven you in all this.
Well, it must be. We have a biblical mandate to heal the sick, feed the hungry, clothe the naked and speak for the oppressed. I'm seventy-five and I've got fewer years ahead than others, so I've got no excuse for not going.

The rarified atmosphere of the House of Lords clearly hasn't detached you from the cold, hard, raw realities of life. However, there is a great gap between those two worlds you inhabit.
There is. But it is a huge privilege to be appointed to the House of Lords. I was not into politics. I was a nurse and social scientist by intention and a baroness by astonishment. I was the first baroness that I'd ever met! It made me wonder how I could use this privilege and be a voice for the voiceless.

It is a great privilege to be able to speak in the House of Lords for those who cannot speak for themselves. As you rightly say, though, they are worlds apart, and so it's sometimes quite difficult making that transition.

I return, maybe, from the jungles of Burma or the killing fields of South Sudan, or from a little Armenian Christian enclave that no one has ever heard of. I have been with people who are suffering great pain. Then I come back to confront governments that could make a difference. Sometimes, for reasons of self-interest or different political agendas, they don't make that difference. So then it's a double agony.

Your appointment as a baroness came thanks to Margaret Thatcher. Why do you think it happened?
After nursing I contracted TB—six months as a patient, the best nursing education anyone can have! Then I went into the academic world and found myself as the head of a department of social sciences in the heady days of the 1970s.

Of the twenty academic staff, sixteen were communists or even further to the left. Their definition of higher education was not mine. Mine is freedom to pursue the truth within the canons of academic rigor. Theirs was hard-line indoctrination, academic blackmail and physical violence.

It was a tough, tough battle which I fought for nine years. Eventually I and two colleagues wrote a book about it all because we knew it wasn't only happening where we were. It was right through the soft underbelly of higher education across much of the United Kingdom. Our book had the uncompromising title *Rape of Reason: The corruption in the Polytechnic of North London.* I was a bit scared, but the day before the book was due to be published, a very famous commentator in the *London Times*, Bernard Levin, phoned me up. (I was getting the kids ready for school!) He said, 'I've just read your book and I think it is the most important book for the future of democracy I've read for ten years. I'm going to cover it in tomorrow's *Times*.'

The book became known, and it got me known. I think that's why Maggie Thatcher gave me a seat in the House of Lords, as a kind of academic freedom fighter.

You went on to found the HART organisation—the Humanitarian Aid Relief Trust—and you have a special passion for two nations

in our region, Burma and East Timor. Considering all the vast needs of the world, why do you go to these places?
To fill a gap. There are very good aid and advocacy organisations around the world like Amnesty International—secular and Christian organisations. But the people for whom I feel a real passion are those suffering oppression and persecution.

They are often not served by major aid and advocacy organisations. That happens because these people are often trapped behind closed borders. Big aid organisations can only get into places with the permission of the sovereign government. If the sovereign government denies access then they can't reach the victims of that government. So those people are left unreached, unhelped and unheard. A lot of the time we are crossing borders illegally and shamelessly to reach out to them.

And you are comfortable with that?
I think it is a moral imperative for Christians to be with the most lost, the last and the least. Obviously you don't do it irresponsibly. You don't do it just to be deviant. You do it to reach people trapped in the jungle, like the people in the war against South Sudan. We went in thirty times to forbidden air strips to take aid to those denied aid—to be a voice for those denied a voice.

Buying the freedom of slaves as you did was not universally welcomed by the anti-slave charities. Why was that?
We were blamed for encouraging the slave trade, but I think that was a complete misunderstanding of the situation. This was not [an example of] economic slavery. This was slavery as a weapon of war—military Islamic *jihad*, 'holy war'. The Khartoum regime rounded up the nomadic tribesmen, gave them horses and

Kalashnikovs and told them they had a duty to go and attack the Christians.

No amount of rescuing them was going to encourage more slavery. It was happening, it was rampant and it was not economic slavery. I do believe we have a moral mandate to set the captive free.

That's incredibly dangerous work.

My word, yes. I was in a village and one night a messenger came to the local tribal chief with this warning: 'We have a force of two thousand Sudanese government soldiers and *mujahedeen.* We are coming at 3.30 in the morning—beware.' I didn't sleep terribly well that night! Unfortunately for the neighbouring village they were diverted there. In the morning the casualties started coming in to us. I'll never forget a brave man who tried to stop the raiders taking boys as slaves. They shot him in the face at point blank range. All the bottom of his jaw was sheered away.

If we hadn't been there those people would have had no aid, no help. That's why it is a moral imperative to be there to free the captive and to help the sick and wounded.

Baroness, elsewhere in the world you have a dialogue under way even with North Korea. Where has that come from and why?

North Korea is probably the world's most closed totalitarian society. Because everyone is meant to worship the Great Leader, there has been an enormous amount of Christian persecution, martyrdom, torture and imprisonment. I and my colleague Lord Alton felt we should visit as parliamentarians to raise our concerns. We applied for visas and, to our amazement, we got them.

It is still illegal to take Bibles into North Korea, but we thought that somehow, being parliamentarians, they just might not examine our luggage. So we took in a lot of Bibles in Korean. On our first visit, every time we had a meeting with [government] ministers, we stood up at the end of the meeting and offered a Bible upside down. We said, 'Your Excellency, this is a very important book in our parliamentary tradition. Back home in the United Kingdom, we begin every day in the House of Lords and the House of Commons with a reading from this book. We would like to give a copy of this book to you as a sign of respect as a fellow parliamentarian.' So we handed over the Bibles and we hoped the host could use them.

And you got away with it!
Well, we left Bibles all over the place, and we hope that the Holy Spirit will be able to use them. One of our mottos is 'It's better to build bridges than walls.' You can use a bridge to cross over and raise your concerns, and raise issues of human rights, religious freedom or religious persecution. There is now a Christian University in Pyongyang. Open up, let a little bit of light in. The light shines in the darkness.

Of all of those that you have worked for and with—those forgotten by most of the rest of the world—is there one particular story that stands out that keeps you fired up to press on?
There are so many; I'll just choose one. It was during the war against the people of South Sudan.

In that war two million perished and four million were displaced. I went there thirty times in the no go areas, walking through the killing fields. I remember landing at one little forbidden airstrip. Whenever we flew in we could see smoke on the horizon from burning villages. Emaciated people would come running up saying, 'Thank God you've come. We thought the world had forgotten us.'

I remember walking through mile upon mile of scorched earth, burnt villages, cattle corpses, human corpses. We came upon one little township that had been attacked about five days before. You could still see the blood on the ground where people had been slaughtered. They had tried to burn the church, but it was a brick church and so it refused to burn. But they chopped the cross off the top and destroyed everything inside.

The pastor, a man named Santino, had been away when the attack took place. He returned to find many of his people killed, including his two brothers. His sister had been taken as a slave. Santino's words I will never forget. He said, 'We Christians here in South Sudan are trying to hold a line against a militant Islamism that wants to move right through South Sudan and throughout the whole of Africa. Khartoum spends $1 million a day on this war. We have nothing and we are trying to hold this frontline of faith. We feel completely forgotten. You're the only Christians who have ever even visited us. Doesn't the church want us anymore?'

Those words turned a knife in my heart. This brave pastor and others like him on those frontlines of faith and freedom today—whether it's Nigeria, Sudan, Egypt or so many other parts of the world—must know that we want them. And not only that we want them but that we cherish them, and that we won't let the price they're paying for our faith be paid in vain.

Colin Buchanan

SONGWRITER, PERFORMER

Colin Buchanan was born in Dublin, Ireland, and moved to Australia when he was six. He's been described as 'simply the best singer/songwriter to emerge in the Australian music scene'.

He trained as a teacher, then went bush with his wife to the Cornerstone Christian Community at Bourke in outback New South Wales. He's a nine times Golden Guitar winner and an APRA and ARIA winner.

Colin has been a presenter on *Play School* and delighted countless numbers of kids (and adults) with his music. Since the mid-1990s he's devoted much of his time to producing albums of Christian music.

Colin's early days in Dublin put an indelible stamp on his musical life.

I do have mental pictures of living in Dublin and church music. I have always loved their folk songs, songs with a story, so maybe floating round there in my mind is 'Paddy McGinty's Goat' or 'Puff the Magic Dragon'.

It was a lovely, secure childhood. I went to a lovely little school that was started by the Quakers and it was a very embracing place.

I felt very much like I was part of a community. Those formative years were really warm, rich, secure and happy.

Why then come to Australia?
Dad lost his job. He was a papermaker. My parents looked at a number of countries where the paper industry was operational. My mum, who's a keen cricket fan, thought, 'Well, if we have to go somewhere, Australia at least has a cricket connection.'

At what stage did you really start to connect with music in your life?
As a kid I walked around the back garden making up songs about what I was doing and just freewheeling. I never had a music lesson as I was growing up. Dad came home with a ukulele one day. To this day I don't know why; it wasn't anyone's birthday or anything like that. We all picked up a few chords on this thing. I liked the thought that I could make up songs.

A lot of people are like that, but not many move on to making it their career. When did that happen?
Bourke and the Cornerstone Community entwined our lives in a really interesting way. I became a Christian as a kid so I have always had a sense of the comfort of knowing God and the sense of destiny in his care for me. I wanted to do things that count for him seeing he was my Lord, mentor, guide and saviour. So our trip to Bourke was very much about making that faith central. Cornerstone was a really great place to do that, but music didn't factor in it initially.

I started writing songs about what I saw and I was getting good feedback. I like playing my songs for people—I like sharing my stories. I gave a couple of tapes to John Williamson when he came through for some shows in 1988. John just said, 'Thanks for that.' The following year a country band called The Flying Emus came through. I really loved their stuff and I gave them a tape. John Kane from the group wrote back and said, 'I love this stuff and I've played it to Festival, my record company.' They said they would like to hear a bit more and it would be great to produce a record. It wasn't big cigars and Cadillacs and stretch limos and all that, but it was an opportunity.

You obviously have a great joy and passion in giving kids a musical life. Why do you think they need that?
I think it's great to remember what it was like to be a kid. (Despite appearances, everyone used to be one!) That lovely secure experience of childhood was my base and I'm really grateful to God and my parents for that. I remember the joy of music and discovering music as a child. I liked hearing stories, and to be able to bring all that to kids is great.

When I was teaching, I would write songs with the class. The first one we did was a chant. These kids would stomp their way out of class and it was lovely. It was their song.

It must be a great thrill when you're performing—to see kids grabbing this and lighting up.
They really do. They are either with you or they're not—there is no middle ground. They are not always polite! If you get them, you get them boots and all, and it's just lively and fun. Because I have a short attention span, I like to entertain myself, and that seems to work for them as well.

It must be a bit of a juggle, though, being the joyous performer you are but also remembering it's a business and career.
I've been really grateful that I haven't had to live on the smell of an oily rag. I've also been a bit repelled by the gratuitous self-promotion that can happen in people's careers. I think that as a Christian I'm someone who has entrusted my life to God, so integrity demands that I live that way. I do that imperfectly, but he must be greater and I must be less. That's a challenge for all of us to take into every sphere of life.

With the business side of it all, sometimes I just wish I didn't have to worry about it. I'm much more interested in writing songs.

What are the ways in which you think your faith has added a richness or depth to your music, either in performing or in songwriting?
There's a great old hymn that says, 'This is my Father's world'. You take a wander through the woods and there he is. Wander through an art gallery and there he is. He's used the abilities of those he's created to weave this incredible richness.

My faith is the goggles through which I look at this world. The fingerprints of God are on every single miraculous, wonderful, beautiful, good thing in this world. So I want that to affect my creativity. That's a fundamental driver for me, and again the credit goes to him. I love it that I serve a Creator.

You are such a joyous, outgoing, happy-go-lucky kind of bloke. How much does that public persona match your private demeanour?
Well, my Year 4 report said, 'Colin is outspoken'! I didn't know what outspoken meant. I brought the report home and my parents had a chuckle. I was the class clown. I was always entertaining myself as much as other people.

So when I dress up in an inflatable chef suit and prance around saying 'Him and Her and You and Me—we need the gospel recipe', it's sort of hilarious. But I really believe that we need the 'gospel recipe'—that's the recipe for life.

Who says you can't have fun in it! Colin, how have your own kids moved with you in this business? I guess it's lots of fun in their early days when they see dad singing and performing. Is there a moment when they cross the line and think, 'Dad, this is so daggy'?
Yes, yes! I guess that's the territory of teens! I also think, though, that our kids have seen us wanting our faith to inhabit the very fabric of our lives. It's been the driving force through all my kid's Christian music. They sense that. They'll still have a bit of a crack, but they are great advocates, which is lovely.

There is a song in one of the film clips I did where they sat on a boat with me and we sang, 'He Died upon the Cross', which is a simple little song with actions. I think my eldest was maybe eight or nine at the time. I've said to them, 'Look, I'm making another DVD now, would you guys sit on a boat and sing "He Died Upon the Cross" again? I know people like to see my kids, and the fact that you've grown up and you bear testimony to that would mean a lot to people.' And they all said yes. They haven't done it yet, but that was a delight to me.

You've won nine Golden Guitar awards as well as ARIAs and APRAs. Is there one highlight in your world of music that you can name?
Slim Dusty has been much lauded and celebrated. I wrote a song about him that's on my latest record, *The Songwriter Sessions*—it's called 'Missing Slim'. I'm struck by how his music penetrated people's lives, just quietly and privately. People could be out fixing

a fence and Slim is on the cassette player coming out of the ute. That's their music and it's about them. I think that's really substantial.

Awards are a great recognition. But the place that your music plays in lives is really significant. Maybe it sounds a bit corny, but it is the greatest reward.

Your musical persona and the work that you do is very well established and very much loved. Is there a private musical persona? Say you're at home on Saturday night with the family or some really good friends—what kind of music would you be putting on?
I've always loved singer-songwriters. Probably the greatest musical joy for me is discovering a great song delivered very simply. That's what keeps you writing too, because you like to think that you might ring the bell from time to time if you hammer hard enough at the carnival!

Colin, there's a lot of the land in many of your songs. Tell us about your affection for the land and your connection with it.
It's nice to come up with words that become a little 'invisible'—that become the springboard for people's impressions. That's another thing I love about songwriting and songwriters. They can propel you into places where you were not necessarily going to go. The most effective songs take you there and just let you go. You become lost in something that is very personal. That's what I hope happens to people when they hear some of my songs about the land.

I think it's a challenge with all the songwriting I've done, especially collaborations, to find new ways of saying things that will keep them arresting and fresh.

Is there a favourite spot in this wide brown land that you love?
I've seen a lot of it. I think the desert is an interesting place because of its impact on me. Initially it seems a bit ugly, harsh and monotonous. It's funny because in the Bible there's a great theme of 'wilderness'. The wilderness is a place of testing, transformation and growth—it makes you small. It's interesting how much bigger you feel after you've been made to feel small.

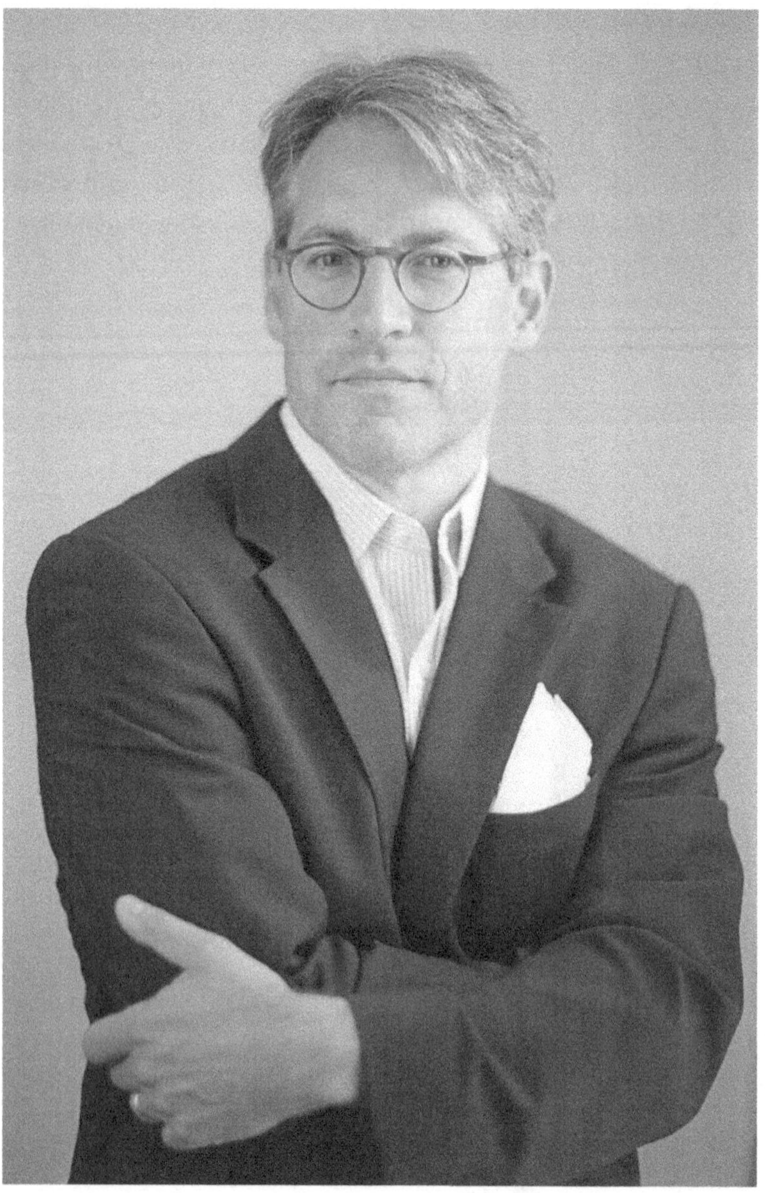

Eric Metaxas

Dietrich Bonhoeffer's biographer

'Dietrich Bonhoeffer's life was of such beauty, courage, integrity and authenticity it is inescapably inspiring—a story that is as eloquent a statement about the meaning of life as anything he could imagine.'

That's the conclusion of Bonhoeffer's biographer, Eric Metaxas. Bonhoeffer lived for just thirty-nine years. He was executed, hanged by the Nazis in the final days of World War 2. Yet he left a vitally important and indelible impression on the Western world, its thinking and especially Christian thought.

Eric Metaxas has broken new ground in his bestselling biography *Bonhoeffer: Pastor, Martyr, Prophet, Spy: A Righteous Gentile versus the Third Reich*.

Most of us have heard of Bonhoeffer, but Eric's book is a rich, intimate and powerful journey through the life of one of the most significant figures of the last century. We began our conversation by exploring Bonhoeffer's early family life.

That was one of the things that really captivated me. This man came from a truly amazing family, there's no denying it. I have never seen such an accomplished group of people. They were all brilliant—geniuses. His father was the most famous psychiatrist in Germany for the first half of the twentieth century.

Everyone in this amazing family was academically ambitious, brilliant and successful, but they were also very kind people. That's what is so interesting. It was the best of liberal and conservative, the best of Christian and secular. It's no wonder that it produced so many heroes. Of course, Bonhoeffer is the most famous, but his other family members were also very, very brave during this period with the Nazis.

His mother was a very serious Christian and went on to home school her children because of her view about the Germany in which they lived.

In a typically German way, they were concerned with right and wrong and what is proper and improper. But there was a lot of grace. It wasn't just legalism about right and wrong. It's hard not to fall in love with the family. It's one of the reasons I put so much of the family into the book.

Bonhoeffer himself becomes an outstanding student and a lecturer in systematic theology in Berlin University at just twenty-five.

Even younger. He gets his doctorate in theology at age twenty-one, which is unheard of. He could write his own ticket, so to speak, in the world of academic theology, but he also wants to be a Lutheran pastor. He wants to preach and teach. He wants to teach Sunday school. He wants to pastor and counsel people. It is a beautiful thing to see this rare combination of gifts.

He could not get ordained until age twenty-five, so he spends a year in Spain as an assistant vicar at a German-speaking congregation. Then he goes to America at age twenty-four, and that's really a famous episode. It's when his faith goes from his brilliant mind down into his heart and he becomes a real disciple of Jesus Christ in a way that he hadn't quite been before.

In New York City, at Union Theological Seminary, an African American student named Frank Fisher from Alabama invites him up to Harlem to visit the Abyssinian Baptist Church. It's a huge African American church and Bonhoeffer is absolutely bowled over by what he experiences that Sunday morning. He's never seen worship like this and never heard music like this. He's never seen a suffering congregation. I think it was literally the largest congregation in America at the time and he saw people who were not playing at religion. They were not merely churchgoers. They were people who seemed transfixed by Jesus, changed by him. The messages from the pulpit were fiery gospel sermons. This was not like anything that he had experienced in any of the white churches in Germany or in New York.

When he goes back to Germany, people can see that he is much more serious about his faith. He is not just a brilliant theologian obsessed with impressing the world with his academic abilities. Rather, he's a disciple of Jesus Christ who seems to take God much more seriously. The Nazis are at that stage rising, so there's this inevitable clash between this changed Bonhoeffer and this changed Germany where people are turning toward Hitler and the Nazis.

He had been raised not to resist the authorities of the day, but that's overturned in his mind by his unfolding approach to 'evil'.

Bonhoeffer is very rare in seeing that the Nazis are not just 'not Christian' but are bitterly and passionately *anti*-Christian. They despised true Christianity and despised true believers in Jesus Christ. They were willing to play patty-cake with the church because the church was in many ways an institution where many people did not really know what they believed. Hitler would play the game of being a Christian and he would instruct his top lieutenants, Goebbels and Goering and all of them, to pretend to be Christian. They needed this to maintain and augment their political power.

Bonhoeffer saw that this was a ruse. The Nazis were instituting many programs and laws which were clearly against the gospel. They prohibited Jews who had accepted Christ from being members of the German church. Bonhoeffer immediately said, 'Wait a minute. God looks on the heart. He doesn't look on your bloodline. He doesn't say, "You have Jewish blood so you cannot be part of the church." The church is the place for everyone.' Eventually he realised that he had to be more active in the actual resistance against Adolf Hitler.

Bonhoeffer is constantly praying and asking the Lord to guide him. His resistance continues to change. Throughout the 1930s he becomes more deceptive with the Nazis. He takes the illegal seminary training he's doing underground. Then the war comes and he realises that he cannot fight in Hitler's war. So in 1939 he decides to go back to America. Many people pulled strings so that he could escape.

But no sooner is he on the ship crossing the Atlantic than he realises he has made a mistake. Somehow he doesn't have the peace of God. He continues to pray asking the Lord to lead him. Every day he is reading the Scriptures, praying, 'Lord, speak to me through these verses, speak to me through your Word, show me what to do.' Every day that passes he is surer and surer that he cannot stay very long in America. He ends up only staying twenty-six days, gets on a ship in New York Harbor and in early July 1939 sails back into what is obviously a dangerous situation.

His friends are astounded that he is there when they see him: 'What are you doing here? We did everything to get you out of here. Now what's going to happen?'

What he did next is where it gets crazy. Bonhoeffer's brother-in-law is a leading member in the conspiracy against Hitler. He is a member of German military intelligence, and he hires Bonhoeffer to use his considerable talents travelling around Europe, ostensibly to further the aims of the Third Reich. In fact, what Bonhoeffer is really doing is joining the top conspirators, who are in military intelligence, in undermining the Nazis and in fact want to assassinate Hitler and his top lieutenants.

At this point Bonhoeffer is travelling around Europe to make secret contact with the Allies and the Churchill government—most notably Anthony Eden—to let Eden and Churchill know that there are Germans inside Germany who are working for the defeat of Adolf Hitler. It is an extraordinary thing, but Bonhoeffer is now a double agent, in fact a spy, even as he looks like he is being a good Nazi.

And he was quite able to justify all that in his own mind, intellectually and theologically, embracing it within his Christian worldview?

I think Bonhoeffer challenges us all to think more deeply, much in the way that Jesus does. You have to think much more deeply than having simple religious slogans about what is right and what is wrong.

Bonhoeffer is in the midst of this evil so he cannot be merely religious. He cannot have easy religious slogans. Ultimately he believes that the Lord has called him to be part of this conspiracy to kill Hitler, to save Germany and the Jews of Germany. He thought these things through from a completely biblical point of view whereas many in the church were not doing that. They had easy religious answers, but Bonhoeffer was asking, 'What is the mind of the Lord? What is the scriptural idea?'

Of course, the easy religious answer is often entirely wrong. It is pharisaical and moralistic. We are supposed to have the mind of Christ and to think more deeply. Bonhoeffer really was calling the church to do that. And that's why the title of the book is *Bonhoeffer: Pastor, Martyr,* Prophet, *Spy*, because there is a prophetic element to his life. He is calling the people of God to be the people of God. He is calling the church to be the church when they really weren't doing that.

Ultimately, though, his secret activities, plotting the downfall of the Third Reich, are found out and he is arrested.

Yes. In fact he was arrested before they found that out. He was arrested in 1943. He had just got engaged, and I tell the story of his love affair and engagement for the first time. He is arrested by the Nazis for his involvement in a plot to get seven Jews out of Germany and into neutral Switzerland to save their lives. I quote many of the letters between Bonhoeffer and his fiancé because they really are quite hopeful that he will fool the prosecutor and get out of jail. Or they are confident that the plotters who are still conspiring to kill Hitler will succeed, or that the Allies will defeat the Nazis and the war will end that way.

Unfortunately, one of the plots to kill Hitler, the Valkyrie Plot, goes awry. And it doesn't just fail to kill Hitler but also exposes the conspiracy. That is the moment, July 20, 1944, when Bonhoeffer's days are numbered. One of the names at the top of the list is Dietrich Bonhoeffer.

He was transferred to some barracks just on the edge of

Buchenwald. On April 8, 1945, Bonhoeffer preached a sermon and conducted a service for his fellow prisoners and then was summoned to go to Flossenburg Concentration Camp. There was an overnight court trial and at dawn he was executed.

He was executed on the express orders of Hitler who simply wanted revenge on the men who had plotted to kill him. You can imagine Hitler in his miserable bunker realising that he's not getting out alive. He's realising that his dream of a Thousand-Year Reich is coming to an end, and thinking in his petty way of the men who worked against him. He was probably thinking that if it hadn't been for their efforts and the efforts of people like them, he would have succeeded. So he was finally a very petty, vengeful man and simply had Bonhoeffer and a few others killed because he wanted them killed—not because he thought he could succeed at that point.

And within days Hitler and the Third Reich are gone and World War 2 is over.

Three weeks later Hitler takes his own life and the Allies win.

I travel widely speaking about Bonhoeffer and I usually end my talks by saying, 'Our instinct is to simply think that this is tragic. If only he could have wriggled free. To die right at the end of the war, to be engaged to be married, aged just thirty-nine and being so brilliant—if only he could have lived a few more weeks.'

But I think Bonhoeffer would have been the first to rebuke us and to say, 'No, I was walking in obedience to the Lord in all of this.' He really believed that and meant to live that way. And if that led him to the gallows then that was the Lord's will, and praise the Lord. He really had a deep faith.

I think that's why the story is so inspiring. It inspires us to have that kind of a faith, to live that way without a fear of death, knowing that God has conquered death. That is really at the heart of why he is so fascinating, so compelling. He is authentic and he is a deeply, deeply faithful Christian. It is hard not be impressed by his faith.

So, Eric, what are we to learn today from this enormously significant figure? What can the church learn? What can we learn personally?
Bonhoeffer makes it clear that Christians must neither avoid politics nor make an idol of politics. God calls us into this dirty world to bring the gospel, to bring salt and light into it. Bonhoeffer is living in a dirty time, an evil time, but he is saying to the church, '*You* must stand up, *you* must perceive what God is saying and *you* must do what God is calling you to do. You are God's hands in the world. If you don't do it, then evil will prevail.'

With regard to how we can live our lives personally, Bonhoeffer shows us that we can live our lives with profound courage. If we really believe what we claim to believe, we will stand for the truth. It gives us the courage and boldness, coupled with the humility of knowing that we are sinners saved by grace.

I think of him as somebody that God has given to us as a model of what it is like to be fully human. What is God's idea of a fully redeemed human being? It is someone who enjoys music and art, laughter and sports, and who couldn't be more serious about God—all rolled into one. It is a beautiful, beautiful picture.

It's not easy in the world in which we live. We need models and we need to see how it can be done. It just makes me happy to be able to bring Bonhoeffer's story before the world at this particular point in time.

Eric, how have you been personally shaped by Bonhoeffer's life and death?

It's made me realise that time is short. A lot of times we think that we will stand up and speak out someday. Bonhoeffer is God's way of saying, 'You must do that *now*; you must be living fully *now*.' Do not shrink from what God calls you to speak. Speak the truth in love, but speak the truth.

I was not a shrinking violet, but I think that something about the story of this brave man galvanises me to be bolder, hopefully in a humble way, to speak the truth.

Sheridan Voysey

'Resurrection Year'

The great untold story of *Open House* has been revealed for the first time. In March 2011, Sheridan Voysey, the man who gave birth to the whole idea of *Open House*, who saw it through to reality and fronted it for five years, walked away from it all, packed up and left Australia.

One big question was left hanging. A few friends and others knew the wrenching reason, but most people and his many, many fans were left wondering: why? Sheridan has now explained it all in his book *Resurrection Year*. His message is simple, a message born out of the wilderness of much pain: that broken dreams can be a chance for a new beginning.

Sheridan joined us from his new home in Oxford in the UK and we began with a love story—how he first met his wife, Merryn.

It all started at the Bible College of Queensland. She would place herself in my path and sit in a particular seat near the college entrance to get my attention. I actually had another girlfriend at the time but things didn't work out with her. When Merryn heard about that, she pricked up her ears and thought,

'Well, maybe there's an opportunity here!' She got my attention, and I'm glad.

Very soon we were off on a three-month camping honeymoon. We had hardly any money, no commitments and a little 1974 Toyota Corolla without air conditioning. We went camping for as long as the money lasted.

Your careers and fields of endeavour are pretty much chalk and cheese.
I've been involved in radio and speaking and writing books, fairly creative things—all about communication. Merryn is a medical statistician and is brilliant with numbers.

So you two fell in love and married, and about three or four years later Merryn raised the subject of having kids. What was your response?
My response was terror, I think! I was an only child for the first thirteen years of my life until my brother came along. By that stage I was a selfish teenager and I wasn't too sure whether this was a good thing or not. Of course I grew to love my brother very rapidly. However, I wasn't too sure whether this whole family thing was for me.

Merryn said, 'I think it's time we started a family.' I was nervous about everything that entailed, but she won me around.

Like so many couples you didn't fall pregnant straight away—and that quickly became quite a big deal for Merryn.
It did. After about six or seven months we went and had some tests done and the tests showed there was a problem on my side. Straight away, of course, that hit at Merryn's soul, because she wanted to be a mum and now that dream was starting to be questioned.

You quickly started to talk about IVF and adoption.
And with that came conversations about the ethics of IVF. That was a difficult one for me, Leigh, because I didn't want to go into IVF without really thinking through the ethical ramifications of it. I wanted to know: is any life lost in the IVF process? If it was we either didn't want to do it, or we wanted to do it in such a way that we avoided that loss of life. I was taking my time trying to work this out and sometimes it was too hard for me and I just gave up.

Merryn was feeling like her whole future was basically waiting on my decision. So you can imagine the tension that started to build in the relationship.

Fast forward about three years and there was still nothing, but you have lots of supportive people around you. Can you tell us about one particular moment with three people—a nun, a missionary and a businessman? They had come to pray with you and lay hands on both of you.
These three wonderful angels started praying for us. Then suddenly—it was a complete surprise to me and to Merryn—I just burst into tears. Merryn had never seen me cry, and here I was sobbing, absolutely sobbing, uncontrollably, gasping for breath. God had walked into the room and he was doing something in me. Lots of stuff came up from my past and it seemed like God was taking that moment to deal with it all.

We left that lounge room that night thinking something supernatural had happened, and, of course, that raised our expectations of a child. However, sadly those expectations were met with disappointment again.

One of the things that so powerfully struck me, as the only other person who knows what this Open House *gig is like to host, was that in the midst of this ongoing anguish you launched this radio program.*
There were a few ironies happening during that time. One was launching *Open House*, a very long-held dream that came to fruition. Also during that time I was approached by Compassion Australia to look after the Compassion Day radio event. Over three years about four thousand children were sponsored through Christian radio stations across Australia under my direction. Right in the midst of Merryn and me trying our hardest to have our own child, we're getting children in the developing world sponsored left, right and centre and having a whale of a time doing *Open House*.

However, there were times when I would arrive on a Sunday night at the studio and Merryn had been in tears again that afternoon. I'd be thinking, 'How on earth am I going to get through another three hours of doing *Open House* after all the stuff that's happening for us personally?'

Sheridan, towards the end of this whole process, there was one final attempt at IVF in December 2010, just a few months before you quit Open House.
We had tried IVF the first time in 2006. We thought we'd give it one more try; if it was unsuccessful it would then be time for us to bring this journey to an end. It had been a ten-year journey by now. And at the last minute it looked like all was well—that Merryn was pregnant. At last it looked like we'd been successful.

You rang your parents to tell them?
Mum squealed and Dad yelled for joy. My brother and my sister-in-law had just a couple of days before announced that they were

pregnant with their second child. So there was jubilation in the Voysey household, I can tell you! People who had been praying for us all these years were texting messages of congratulations to us in tears.

However, sadly, on Christmas Eve 2010, we received a phone call from the IVF clinic. 'We are so sorry,' they said, 'it was a false alarm.' Merryn put down the phone, walked into the bedroom and curled up into a foetal position. That was the way our journey of trying to start a family ended.

Around that same time there was one friend who, no doubt driven by a good heart, came to pray for you and said this: 'Believe God for this pregnancy.' It seemed to me that he was saying, 'If you have enough faith this will happen.' He was putting it, in a way, back on your shoulders.
Yes. And as you said, he was very well meaning.

My response was that I just didn't have energy left for that. I'd tried that. By the time we were at the end of this ten-year journey, we had prayed our hearts dry, and so had other people. I simply said, 'If this is going to be down to my faith, we can pack up now and go home, because I've got nothing left.' What kind of God would disqualify us at the end because we didn't have stamina for the journey?

Not long before this you had a very significant conversation with the author Adrian Plass.
I had interviewed Adrian a number of times over the years and this time we also spoke off-air. He asked how I was and what the New Year held. Adrian is a very caring fellow, and he is able to draw things out of you simply because he listens. I said, 'Well, it's been a tough year and we're right in the midst of a tough time. I don't

know what 2011 is going to hold, but I hope it's going to be better than this year.'

I didn't tell Adrian the whole story, but I told him enough for him to say this: 'In the Christian scheme of things, new life follows the death of something, just as Jesus' resurrection followed his crucifixion. After what you've told me, Sheridan, I think you and Merryn could do with a Resurrection Year.' I went home and told Merryn what Adrian had said and she burst into tears. But these weren't tears of sadness; they were tears of joy.

Sheridan, tell us the kind of things that were going on in your mind in the conversations between you and Merryn about leaving both Open House *and Australia.*

There came a moment when Merryn asked if we could move to Europe. I thought, 'Go to Europe? There are lot of very good things happening for me right here in Australia.' That was a difficult conversation to have. Merryn just wanted to get away and start again somewhere—to have a new experience to wipe the slate clean. That was going to be a huge cost to me because it would mean leaving *Open House*. It would mean leaving some exciting opportunities to speak at conferences, and it would jeopardise my publishing options too. As you well know, Leigh, the big thing with publishing is for an author to have a 'profile'—a platform, a following of readers. I had that in Australia, but I didn't have it in Europe. All I could think of was the cost.

I'm struck by what a gift that ends up being for Merryn after such a decade, but there was also a distinct possibility that your departure was going to be the end of Open House.

Our manager, Phil, and I had a conversation. He said, 'Look, it may be that *Open House* has to close as a result of you leaving.' That brought heartbreak upon the heartbreak. He said it wasn't so much about finding somebody who could do the job but about the nature of radio. It's a very personal medium, and if a show is built around a particular personality and you lose that personality, the question is whether the show can continue on. That was the conversation we had, and thankfully that was well before the conversation began with you, Leigh.

And that opened a big new door for both of us, I'll tell you! On that very memorable night of the big handover on your final program, when all the goodbyes were said and the photos were taken, I remember such a feeling of goodwill in the air. What was it like to go home after that?

When I got home there was firstly a sense of exhaustion. It was the next day that it all really hit me. I thought, 'This is it, Sheridan—you're washed up, you're forgotten.' I had a meeting that day with a publisher and he said, 'Oh, you've left *Open House*?' The sentiment was clear: publishers are looking for that profile and platform, and I had lost it, making my prospect of publishing with them unclear.

It was a hard time because there was that crushing sense of 'who am I now?' I have to say, Leigh, that that is a good thing to go through because I don't think we should ever build our identities on a particular ministry, whether it be a radio program, a church or whatever. Our identity should always be in the fact that we are children of a living God who loves us. Nothing can shake that—nothing can take that away from us. So in some sense leaving *Open House* was a bit of a gift, having some of those false notions of identity stripped away.

There is great wisdom in that. I'm also struck by the total turnaround in the circumstances of you and Merryn. You're going through that and she's now saying that your next chapter has to be 'fun, restful and an adventure'. You both clearly felt it was OK to do a bit of self-care. That's another good lesson and a bit of wisdom for many of us. It's OK to look after yourself.

Indeed! There was a time in my life when I was a very 'angsty' Christian, and this wouldn't have been a natural thing for me to think back then. I would have felt guilty if we had a bit of time-out, a bit of rest, a bit of play.

No, God is a good God, and there may well be a time when you need a Resurrection Year, or at least a resurrection month or a resurrection week—where you simply go and have some fun. God's got a huge world out there, full of colour, full of play and all sorts of things that will help restore you. That was going to have to be part of our Resurrection Year. It was time for a rest, and not least because of the grief that had gone on just before it.

So you headed off, doing some wonderful things through Europe on the way to Merryn starting a new job in Oxford. I'm wondering if you were suffering 'relevance deprivation syndrome'.

We had really great times travelling through Europe. It was when we got to Oxford that it really hit me. Merryn left the wilderness to enter the Promised Land of Oxford, coming to this amazing job at Oxford University. But that's when I started to sit at home while she went to work and say to myself, 'OK, what's my life to be now?'

Of course, Merryn had faced her own questions—particularly about why God hadn't given us a child, and why he'd remained silent for so long about it to us. The question about God and suffering has been the great question of the ages. We still don't have any clear-cut answers on that because it's very, very hard to find them. However, after some time studying, thinking and praying about it all in Switzerland on the way to the UK, Merryn came to a point of thinking maybe God wasn't as mean as she had started to think he was. That was a big move.

In the words of Phillip Yancey, 'When God is silent, it doesn't mean he doesn't care.'
Indeed. God is sometimes silent, but that doesn't mean he's absent.

Then came another very significant hook-up between you two and Adrian Plass and his wife, and that was where the idea for a Resurrection Year became the idea for a book.
In that conversation off-air in November 2010, Adrian had said if we ever came through the UK we should come and stay with him and Bridget. They were at the time based in North Yorkshire at a place called Scargill House, which is like a retreat centre.

The full story of our ten-year walk in the wilderness of infertility came out when we visited them there. On the Saturday night of our visit, Adrian and I were sharing a glass of sherry. The girls had gone to bed, and he and I were talking about publishing. And he said, 'Have you thought about writing your story into a book?' I said, 'What do you mean, like a memoir?' I didn't know if I really wanted to write a book on infertility—I didn't want to be known as the infertility guy. He said, 'It's not a book about infertility. Your story is much bigger than that. Your story is about broken dreams and holding on to God even when he doesn't make sense to you. It's about starting again, having a new life after the death of something. I know many people would benefit from reading a book like that.'

I still wasn't sure, but the idea wouldn't leave me. Half an hour later or so I said, 'This book idea of yours—wouldn't 'Resurrection Year' be a great title for it?' He said, 'Yes, actually, it would!'

I wasn't sure whether Merryn would want to share our story as she's a private girl. And remember, we hadn't told anybody our story apart from very close friends, because it's a vulnerable story. Well, Merryn prayed about it. We both prayed about it. And more and more it just seemed like this was the right thing to do.

So here we are. I've written a book about our story called *Resurrection Year*. I never thought we would be sharing this story publicly.

Who would you like to see tap into this book, Sheridan? What would you like them to get out of your and Merryn's story?
This book is for anybody who has experienced a broken dream. That might be the couple who have had a very similar journey to ours of being unable to start a family. It might be the single girl or guy who's always longed to be married but the right person has never come along. It might be the person whose career hasn't taken off the way they wanted it to, or the person who has lost their career.

By the time we reach our thirties and forties, most of us have a broken dream. Maybe we've lost a child. Maybe we were able to have a child but not have a second child. Merryn and I don't have any simple answers for you. We don't have 'five steps' that will fix up your life. Life is a lot messier than that, and God is a lot more mysterious than that. He takes us through these difficult times because he wants to build us into somebody new. There is a new beginning after a broken dream if you walk with God through it.

I never wanted to share this story, but it's amazing the healing that is starting to come as people read this book. It's like God is redeeming the pain we've gone through by us simply sharing our story so that others can feel they're not alone. As people read *Resurrection Year*, they come to realise that they can have a new beginning too.

103.2

Tim Dixon

POLITICAL MINDER AND SOCIAL ACTIVIST

Tim Dixon knows what it's really like to dwell in the inner sanctum of power and politics in Australia. He knows what it's like to move into the Prime Minister's suite on the back of Kevin Rudd's sweeping victory of 2007 and see all that so suddenly collapse in tears some two-and-a-half years later.

He also knows what it's like to straightaway begin working with Julia Gillard as Australia's first female Prime Minister. In fact, Tim Dixon has worked closely alongside three Labor leaders—and also knows what it's like to have a much bigger picture in a life grounded by faith in an all-powerful God.

These days Tim works in New York with *Purpose.com*, aiming to bring about the kind of change in the world that politics alone just can't achieve. Speaking with Tim, I couldn't help but wonder if we were listening to a possible future prime minister!

One of the lessons that I've gained from working in politics is that there are a lot of people in government who want to do really good things, but they're not as powerful as you think from the outside. From the inside you realise that they are constrained by many things. A lot of politicians nowadays are very reactive rather than proactive.

If we're going to achieve big changes we really need a groundswell of public support. Otherwise the special interest groups, who are always there, will block good things that can be done.

Purpose is basically there to do that kind of work—to build the public support and public engagement around a whole lot of complex issues.

I don't think politicians are any longer in the position to do that in the way they once did because people don't like them and don't trust them. When a community movement starts and drives an issue, however, people are much more willing to listen and engage. That's the kind of work that Purpose does.

Social media is a very important part of that.
It's critical. The technology enables us to engage people in ways that were never possible before. Social media empowers ordinary people to be involved. You don't have to be part of a political party, or in parliament, or even in a formal organisation or institution. I think that is one of the exciting points of our time, that power can be spread out more.

If our leaders, as you say, can't lead as they once did, how do you define what good government is and what good leadership is?
The essence of good leadership is having integrity as an individual, but integrity also in terms of your values. Politicians talk a lot about values, but to me the real test of your values is, 'What are you prepared to pay a price for?'

There's a price for pushing for things that are not popular. And today it is so much harder to have a conversation with the public and engage. Everything gets reduced to 140 characters on Twitter.

So there is a dumbing down of debate and it's hard to break

through that. That's where I think online social movements can play a role, building a larger debate where the politicians can't.

Was the kind of work you've done in politics and Purpose always in view when you chose economics as your specialty?
I've always had a passion for the big issues of politics and how the world works. And for some reason I got fascinated reading newspapers, even as a kid in primary school, which my parents thought was deeply strange.

You sad individual! How did your Christian faith inform all that mix?
Very significantly, because I've always sensed, at a personal level, the importance of integrating all the different parts of life. If God transforms individuals, then surely that also has a larger social impact and a larger effect on society. Faith is never purely a private thing. It obviously has enormous ramifications in your personal life, but I think historically that when God works—well, look at periods of revival; they have larger social effects. I've always tried to understand how those pieces fit together.

While I share your concern about that, how do you bring faith into the public policy realm in a way that doesn't develop into that muscular dogmatism for which public Christianity is often known?
This is where I reckon we need to do better theology. I think if the Bible is describing all of life and all of reality, then it surely offers a whole lot of insights into what makes society work, what fulfils human beings and what our responsibilities are to each other. It always puzzles me that debate is often so narrow—about personal conduct and those sort of classic personal morality issues.

All the same, are you able to convince the politicians of that kind of worldview? Are you able to convince the media? Both sides are so focused on the polls every week or fortnight.

I don't need to engage in Trinitarian theology with Julia Gillard, and I think she would fall asleep if I tried! But there is no doubt to me that there are many points of public policy in Australia where people know that we are at a dead end. Policy approaches we are using aren't working. I've had this conversation with some cabinet ministers in the last few years, and they say, 'Look, we're trying this, we're trying that, but we know that none of these things are really working.' So we kind of resign ourselves and say we do the best we can.

Today there is more of an opening for fresh ideas. I think we are in a very different environment to where we were thirty or forty years ago when there was a very hard demarcation about secular government. Christian people were seen as religious zealots. Now there is much more opening if you come forward with an idea and say, 'Why don't we try this? Let's look at what's happening at a local community level.' Government is not the solution to all of those things. I think there is a real opportunity to look into new ways of approaching old problems, and those can come out of Christian insights.

Tim, you've worked with three Labor leaders. Why Labor and not conservative politics?

All of the political parties have traditions and cultures. I have friends across all the parties personally, but the heart of what made the Labor Party is its belief in social justice. The commitment to giving opportunity and advancement to people who don't have opportunities is very much the heart of the gospel message and very much the heart of the biblical story.

The interesting part of the Labor Party's history, lost to most people, is that it very much grew out of Methodism. Methodism drove the trade union movement and was very influential in the early days, so the idea that your faith would lead you into Labor politics seems to me to be quite natural.

I do appreciate that over the last few years there is almost an expectation that people of Christian faith are likely to be conservative voters, and the numbers certainly show that. To me, and to lots of Christians I know, especially younger people, it feels just as natural to be in the Labor Party. So that perception might change in the next few years.

How do you see the Labor Party holding on to and representing those founding principles?

All of the modern political parties have the struggle of sustaining their foundational values and translating them in the modern era. I think the Labor Party has warts all over it, as we do individually. One of the elements of politics that I think is problematic is the need to always conform and to pretend there are no disagreements.

The Labor Party in government has made many mistakes and has disappointed many of us in many different ways, but equally it has accomplished a great deal. In Australia we have a parliamentary democratic system where you're either going to end up on the left or the right. That's the institutional structure—let's make it work as best we can.

I would equally wish the very best for friends who go to the other side of politics, and then I'll debate the issues vigorously, yet respectfully.

The first Labor leader you worked with was Kim Beazley. Paint us a picture of him as a man and as a leader.
Kim is a lovely guy in terms of his personal faith. He's an immensely likeable, warm, charitable person and someone who was very easy to work with.

I remember one moment when we were giving a speech to a Christian audience and I sat down with him. I said, 'I think you should be talking about your personal faith.' We had this long, very personal conversation which seemed extremely strange because we were in the middle of a political party conference! Kim had an amazing ability to forget everything—all the craziness going on outside. He started reciting to me 'When I Survey the Wondrous Cross' and gave me the entire hymn. I thought it was quite remarkable.

So feeling that kind of affection for a bloke like Kim Beazley, was it a hard thing when you saw Kevin Rudd knock him off and suddenly had to work with Kevin Rudd?
The day itself was really hard because Kim literally walked out of the Caucus vote and was told that his brother had died. Kim's staff were close to him, so the combination of those things, I think, was quite devastating.

Politics has many intense moments like that and that was certainly an intense moment. But at the end of the day you're very committed and you do your job, and you try to do it as best you can. Ultimately you're working for the country's best interest and for the party. Kevin came and we moved on.

It was well known behind the scenes that you shared a very personal connection with Kevin Rudd, beyond what's typical with politicians and their staffers—and that was that faith connection.
Kevin is a peculiar animal because he does literally sit up till two o'clock in the morning reading obscure German theology.

So it's true!
It is actually true. Kevin is a multi-coloured personality.

I'll preface this question by saying that none of us is perfect—our public profession of faith does not always match our private behaviour. How then did you process or deal with the public Kevin as against the private Kevin, who we have heard so much about over the last few years?
I'd say this: you work with people and you try and bring out their best. I don't think I have a deep understanding of Kevin. He has terrific aspirations and deep values, but he's also someone who, on a bad day, shares his bad day with everyone else. So we all hope that there are more good days!

Kevin is neither the demon that some people claim nor the saint that others would say he is. He's a human being, flesh and blood like all of us.

It's very hard for us to genuinely understand the extent of the pressure and how that weighs on an individual, so in that respect I feel like we have to cut our political leaders a break and not focus on a lot of irrelevant personal information.

I'm sure that Kevin would be the first person to say he had lessons to learn from his time in office. Politically I guess he paid the price for that.

I think as a Christian, biblically, the test of good leadership is much more to do with what you do in office and how that affects the people you govern.

So with the depth and intensity of the connection you had with him, on the day when that all ends so suddenly in tears, how do you pick up the pieces and then start working with Julia Gillard?
I had also worked with Julia very closely since 2007. I had a lot of respect for her and really liked her. She is a very easy person to work with and a very good manager.

When you're a staffer, you're not an elected official. You're not an elected member of parliament. You are not responsible ultimately for the decisions about who is the leader of the party. You accept that's not your role. My role is to serve the leader, serve the party and serve the nation. And leaders often look different publically to who they really are.

Tim, you emerged from this searing hothouse of politics, especially from that inner sanctum, with a range of incredibly valuable insights, experiences and abilities that I think would be hard to gain anywhere else. I'm sure you've learnt a lot about people and how to deal with them, and about relationships.
Yes, and I guess it's partly informed by personal faith and believing in the dignity of every person and in the value of respect—working with each person to bring out their best.

I'm often struck, in an odd way, by the everyday practicalities of human beings. For instance, in the midst of great moments of national crisis or urgency, one of the most significant things you can do is go out and buy a coffee for everybody else who's working late into the night!

Tim, I have one burning question in speaking with you: is there a job in politics for you? Do you have any ambition for that?
Personally I have a strong sense (and it comes out of my faith) of

'calling' to work in the public sphere—to work on these large issues of justice and overcoming injustice. Right now the work I'm doing is richly stimulating and rewarding.

I'm certainly interested in the longer term in getting into politics in an elected role. But after seeing the downside of it all, I know it's so immensely costly in terms of peoples' lives and families. I don't see much glamour in it—it's a real grind.

I also think it is really wrong to think that it's the only way, or even the main way, that someone can contribute to making a better society. I think there are so many other ways—including business, social enterprise, church leadership and community leadership. So that's the calculation for me, to weigh up those things and prayerfully consider it. I guess I'll make that decision sometime in the next few years.

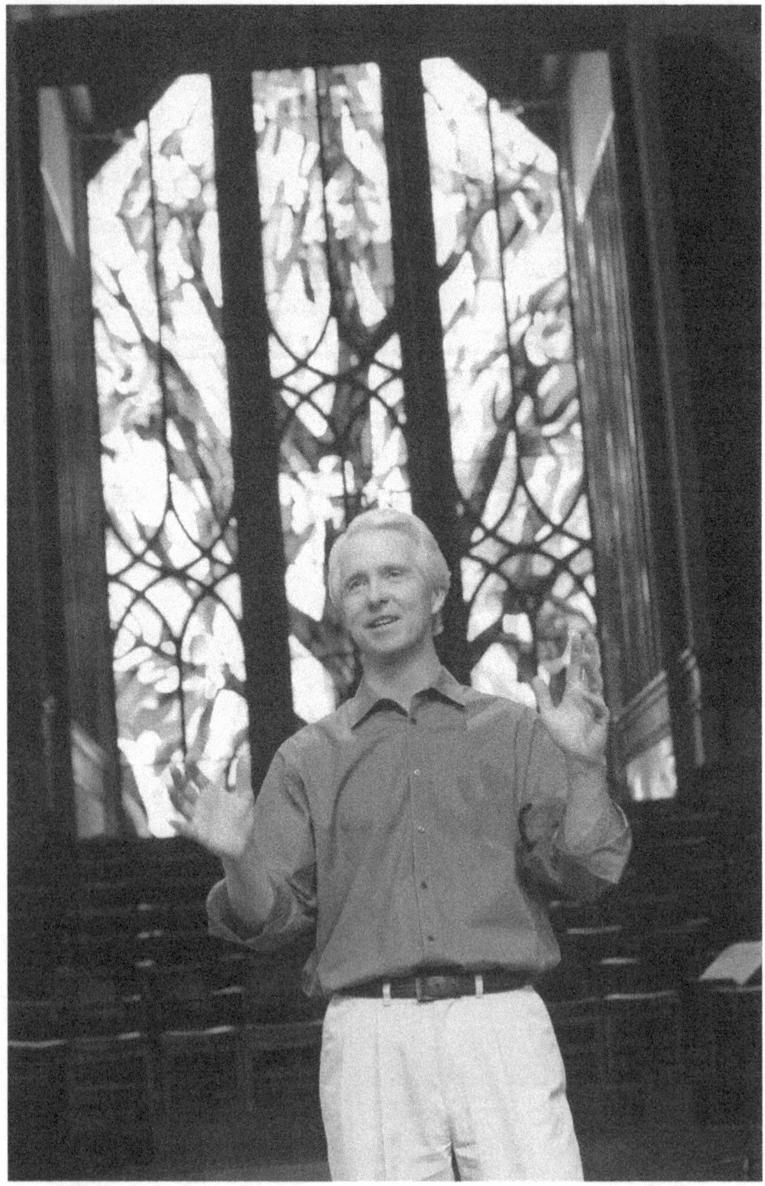

John Ortberg

Who is this man Jesus?

John Ortberg is one of my favourite communicators and 'podcast preachers'. He has a PhD in clinical psychology, he was a pastor at Willow Creek Community Church in the US, and for the last decade he has headed up Menlo Park Presbyterian Church in the San Francisco Bay area.

John is a prolific author, with books like *If You Want to Walk on Water, You've Got to Get Out of the Boat* and *Everybody Is Normal Till You Get to Know Them.*

Former US Secretary of State Condoleezza Rice has written a forward to John's latest book. In it she says, 'It gives those who believe and those who are perhaps not so certain a compelling reason to seek answers about this man Jesus.' The book is *Who Is This Man? The unpredictable impact of the inescapable Jesus.*

I began our conversation by asking John to name the best thing and the most challenging thing about his job.

The best thing about it is the hope. I cannot imagine doing life outside of Jesus—his life, his teachings, his story. To be in a universe where there is a person like that is the best part about it.

The most challenging: I'm somebody who has a lot of doubts and a lot of questions. My mind just works that way. There are things that I feel I don't understand, like suffering. I don't get why people have to suffer the way they do. I have a list of questions that I want to talk to God about.

Embracing Christian faith is one thing; it's an entirely different thing to move from clinical psychology to ministry. How and why did that happen?

Two reasons. One is that I was a horrible therapist! When I was going through the program, I found when people came to see me for therapy they would get worse! I felt really stressed in the process—that if I had to do this for the rest of my life I'd just slit my wrists now!

At the same time I started to work at a church. I began to preach and found that I loved the church and loved to preach. I loved being part of a team and part of that kind of a community. It was really a lack of effectiveness and joy in one field and a deep sense of joy and calling in another one.

Following on from that, how important is it for you to truly love the people to whom you preach, as well as being their teacher and leader?

I asked the great Dallas Willard (who was kind of a mentor for me), 'Why should people go to church? What's the most important reason to go to church?' His answer surprised me. I thought it would be something theological or something about worship or even about learning. What he actually said was, 'The most important reason to go to church is to find people to love—it's to be with people and love them. We can do many other things on our own, but the church really is people.'

I've come to the conclusion that that's true for me as well. I do love to teach and I love to think, and there's also a part of me, for better and worse, where I come alive in front of a group of people. Communicating with them activates me. So the danger for me is that preaching can simply be about ideas and performance. My primary calling is to love people. I know when I get to the end of my life, Leigh, that what will make a difference and what will count is the people I've loved. Training people to love people is actually on the top of my list these days.

So to your book about Jesus, who you say is the most influential man in the world. As you admit, he's also a man who's hard to know when we can't see or touch him.

Jesus had an enormous impact on the world and the history of the world—on education, on political thought, on the expression of compassion, on how we view children, on art. They are all fundamentally different for most of us than they would be if Jesus had not been born.

Even folks inside the church, even folks familiar with the Bible, often have simply no idea of the size of the wake that he left behind in his life. Whether or not somebody believes that Jesus was divine, we live in a profoundly Jesus-shaped world.

One of the many striking things about his life is that his impact was greater one hundred years after his death than during his life—and it's gone on and on from there.

With most people who have a big influence on the world, you knew on the night they died that they were going to be famous. You knew their name would reverberate through history—people like Caesar Augustus, Alexander the Great, or Steve Jobs for that matter.

When Jesus died, on that night he only had a tiny, obscure handful of followers in a middle-ranked city tucked away in the Middle East. Nobody could have predicted that he would have such an impact on the world. It's not simply that he's had a greater influence than anybody else that's so striking. It's the gap between how unlikely that impact would have seemed compared with the impact he has had on the world in reality.

So how do you account for such an influence over thousands of years?

Part of what I do in the book is talk about Jesus in a way that could be accessible for somebody who doesn't know if they believe in God. I say, 'Let's just take a look at how our world is different because he lived. If you do, you might find that pretty soon you become an admirer of his. Then if you keep admiring him enough, eventually you might want to start trying to do the work that he did. You might ultimately end up becoming a believer.'

I actually think it's very difficult to look deeply at his life and impact and not end up believing that there is something beyond the merely human in this man's existence.

This movement didn't happen with political or military power, forcefully or loudly. How did it spread?

It captured human minds and imagination like no other philosophy, no other person and no other teaching. In the ancient world, humility was not a widely admired virtue. People thought if somebody was great they ought to be really puffed up about it. In fact, the Australian historian John Dickson has written a book called *Humilitas*. He says the primary reason humility became an admired virtue in the world was because of the life of Jesus and the cross.

When it comes to the idea of forgiveness, or love of enemies, there's a similar clash of thought in the ancient world. They thought you should help your friends but get revenge on your enemies. It was through Jesus that this notion of forgiveness and love of enemy spread through the wider world. Over and over and over he had this kind of impact.

Can I ask you about one particular aspect of Jesus' ministry and his work? What did he mean to the women of his day?

A lot of folks don't understand how difficult and cruel the ancient world could be for women. In the ancient world there were about 1.4 million men for every 1 million women. When you ask what happened to those other 400,000 women, they were simply born the wrong gender and were left to die of exposure right after birth. That's the world into which women were born. They were very commonly sold into slavery and that almost always involved sexual exploitation. In ancient Rome this was not a source of embarrassment—it was literally glorified.

The sexual behaviour of men and the restrictions around women were something that everybody knew and understood. Women for the most part were not educated.

It was largely Jesus who changed all that—the way he dealt with women, the way he treated them, included them and taught them.

You read through the apostle Paul's letters and see that an extraordinary number of women are cited in leadership positions within the church. Women flocked to the church in its early centuries in disproportionate numbers. Those who were fined for surviving their husbands in ancient Rome were cared for in the early church. It took a long time and the church often got it wrong, but Jesus and his movement ended up elevating and changing the way women were viewed and treated in the world in staggering ways.

And for women, as for all people, at the very heart of his 'new command' is love. How do you reflect on the place of love in Jesus' life and how that went on to shape the world?

Leigh, that's a great observation. That God is a God of love was again not a common idea in the ancient world. For instance, nobody ever said, 'I love Zeus!'

The notion that God is a loveable being who wants to be loved is actually an idea that came out of little Israel: 'Hear, O Israel, the Lord your God, the Lord is one. Love the Lord your God with all your heart and with all your soul and with all your strength.' That God is love came from Israel through Jesus to the rest of the world. He didn't just teach it, he lived it.

Every time somebody says 'I believe in a God of love', they are remembering, knowingly or not, one more of the gifts that Jesus has given us.

And yet you also say Jesus is a dangerous man, which seems a surprising thing to say.

A lot of times the perception that people have of Jesus is that he is a very sensitive person—that he's very gentle, that he likes to hang out with children and you see sheep around him. Yet at the same time we're told that he went into the temple and overturned tables. Not only that, he got a whip and drove people out of the temple. When we ask ourselves 'What would Jesus do?', we don't often think, 'Oh, he'd get a whip and turn tables over.'

Jesus' commitment was to God. He cared for every person and for justice. This meant that when injustice was done—say, when there was a person who was diseased and people who claimed to be religious didn't want to heal them because it was the Sabbath—Jesus would deliberately make things extremely uncomfortable for those religious leaders. He was a very dangerous guy for people with power who would exclude or demean or cheapen the humanity of others. That got him into enormous trouble and eventually got him killed. His movement also meant enormous trouble for people who had power and would abuse it.

John, there's one particular word you highlight in your book—the word 'hypocrite'. You note this word occurs seventeen times in the New Testament, frequently from the lips of Jesus. Of course, hypocrisy

is a great barrier to faith today. Why do you focus in on that particular word?
You'll often hear folks complain about hypocrisy in the church and Christians who are hypocrites. Very often that's extremely well deserved. There can be an enormous amount of hypocrisy.

But it was Jesus who focused attention on the word hypocrite. The old Greek word *hypokrites* was used for actors who would wear a mask. Jesus is the primary person who gave the word its moral content and shaped it to talk about how faith aims at producing a transformed heart. People who try to make their behaviour look good while their hearts are bad are the folks he called hypocrites.

So ironically, even when people complain about religious hypocrisy, they're actually paying a tribute to Jesus, who himself condemned religious hypocrites.

So if he's the man who's hard to know without seeing and touching him, how do we find out about him—and, if we do, what will we find?
There's that wonderful little phrase at the beginning of the gospel of John where one man is talking to another man about Jesus. The invitation that he offers is 'come and see'. You might have questions, you might have doubts and you might be sceptical, but just come and listen to what he says, look at the way he lives and try to do what he teaches. See what happens.

I would say it's the greatest invitation that has ever been offered to the human race. It has changed lives in every culture and every century, and it still does.

I suggest that you actually start with the New Testament. Go back to the gospel of Matthew and the gospel of John and look at the way that Jesus treated people. Look at how his life was lived and then read what he taught. Read about the 'golden rule', read about how to handle anger, how to handle money, how to handle lust, how to be anxious for nothing. Take him as your teacher and try to live what he says. I think people will go from being students of his to admirers of his, then followers and believers.

Judith Durham

THE VOICE OF THE SEEKERS

It's a little known fact that Judith Durham's career, which has now spanned more than fifty years, began with a prayer that her mother said before Judith was even born. Who could ever have imagined what would follow?

In 1965 Judith sang 'The Carnival Is Over' with her fellow Seekers, Athol Guy, Bruce Woodley and Keith Potger. It was at the height of Beatlemania, with the Rolling Stones at full throttle. That Seekers' song outsold both the Beatles and the Stones and remains in the UK's Top 100 best-selling singles of all time.

Judith joined us on *Open House* in the lead-up to a new series of reunion concerts celebrating fifty years of the Seekers. Sadly, the tour was interrupted mid-way through when Judith suffered a brain haemorrhage. She is now recovering.

We began a rich conversation with that prayer her mother prayed.

She didn't want her baby to be tone deaf and it was the same with my sister too. Beverley also is a wonderful singer. It's amazing to think what that has brought about for me. It's a gift from somewhere.

Music was very important to my mother and to Dad. They sacrificed a lot so that my sister and I could have piano lessons.

You went on to study music at quite a high level throughout your childhood.

Yes, I did, thanks to Mum and Dad. I'll never be able to thank them in my heart enough. I had eleven years of classical piano and I ended up studying with Professor Ronald Farren-Price at the University of Melbourne. I actually got my AMusA and I did carry on for a year after that, but singing had really started to take over my life. I didn't have the time to dedicate to the practice I really should have been doing.

The realisation is hitting me more and more that my parents equally gave a huge amount of value to my musical tuition simply by buying sheet music for me. They realised that I was a very, very keen sight reader (once I understood about sight reading). That was my huge treat. I didn't want lollies or toys. I just wanted sheet music so I could play more and more tunes.

It was a huge adventure. I just wanted more and more difficult music. It was the fun of seeing what came out of the printed dots on the page that gripped me. We didn't have a record player so all of the tunes were virtually unknown to me. I am so grateful to my parents.

And then you were drawn to jazz, Dixieland and gospel. What was it about those styles, or the people associated with them, that attracted you?

I was still intending to study for opera or musical theatre, but trad jazz, Dixieland and gospel were all the rage. Pre-Beatles, the dances where all the young people went were either rock 'n' roll or trad jazz—traditional, vintage, Dixieland jazz. The interesting thing about it is how much it drew on gospel music. I knew of Negro spirituals, as we used to call them, and I enjoyed singing them, and I had some hymn books from our family's history, so I used to love singing anything that was religious. However, it didn't have the beat that jazz music had. That was a big change for me—to see how African American people would interpret music, with the wonderful gospel message, of course. They were happy because they were truly getting that message and understood the joy of it all, and expressing it in a style I had never known.

That was when I was eighteen. I was listening to the blues of Bessie Smith and the gospel music of Mahalia Jackson and Sister Rosetta Tharpe. When I joined the Seekers, Keith introduced me to some of the gospel quartets, like the Spirit of Memphis quartet. They had really beautiful harmonies, but that infectious rhythm that gave the music huge joy was amazing.

We have had so many conversations on Open House *with a wide range of musicians who have seen the powerful impact that gospel music has had on lots of other genres of music.*

Without a doubt. I sang for about a year with various jazz bands, and the high spot for me was with Frank Traynor's Jazz Preachers, singing tunes like 'We Shall Not Be Moved', 'Just a Closer Walk with Thee' and 'Open Up Them Pearly Gates'. I was singing those songs in my jazz sets just about every night of the week.

When I then joined up with the Seekers—which was a very, very casual introduction to them, just for fun initially—I found that some of the songs I'd been doing would suit the group perfectly. So it all crossed over: the folk world, the gospel world and the trad-jazz world. And, of course, the classical world before that.

That wonderful influence of gospel and spirituality crossed over through all of them.

I believe you began your singing career one night at a jazz club when you simply asked to get up and sing.
Yes, I did. I had to be a bit persistent. They turned me away the first time I asked. I was very straight-laced, born and bred to be a very polite young lady, and of course I was classically trained. So I didn't look at all like a singer.

What made you ask?
Just the thrill, the infectious quality of the music. I just wanted to have the experience of singing with that musical backing. It was a complete turnaround. And bear in mind I was about to start learning opera. Within two months I was booked with a singing teacher to have my voice classically trained. So this was my moment to have a go at singing this other style of music.

And forget the opera!
To be quite honest, Mum was worried that I was going to strain my voice. In fact, she took me along to speak to June Bronhill backstage. She was starring in *The Sound of Music* at the time, at the Princess Theatre. I very sheepishly walked into June Bronhill's dressing room. She was very, very kind to see me like that, and she said, 'Look, be very, very careful—you could well strain your voice.' It was pretty loud music.

So this meeting with Athol Guy, Bruce Woodley and Keith Potger was a very casual kind of introduction?
Oh, it was indeed. I don't necessarily believe things happen by

coincidence—I believe in the divine hand. Mum was concerned that I wasn't earning enough money as a secretary, so I went along for an interview at a place called J. Walter Thompson, not even realising it was an advertising agency. When I got out of the lift and saw 'advertising' I thought, 'Oh dear, they're not going to want me.' Anyway, I thought, 'Oh well, I'm here now, I might as well go in'—and the market research manager gave me the job as his secretary.

When I arrived there I told all the girls on the first day that I was singing with jazz bands, and they said, 'There's another singer working in this office. His name is Athol Guy—one of the account executives.' So I bowled up and said, 'Hi, I'm Judy Durham', and he said, 'I've been meaning to come and hear you—why don't you come along tonight and have a bit of a sing with us?' (He was singing with Keith and Bruce.)

I thought, 'Oh well, I've got nothing to lose.' So Bruce came and picked me up, and they were all absolutely gorgeous. I didn't know whether I would fit in because I was so 'plain Jane'. Anyway, it was great and lots of fun. I sang harmonies where I could and I did the odd little solo. Every Monday night I would do that with the boys.

Do you reckon it clicked with them from that first night?
It did, yes. And you'll never guess who has told us since that he was in the audience with his parents on that night. At eight years old, under one of the tables, was Clive Palmer, the mining magnate! Isn't that brilliant?

Judith, can you put into words the delight that it was to be up there singing with those three men when it started to really click and then fire?
There was no doubt a buzz. There was always a buzz in those days, even though the audiences were reasonably small. It's interesting

that we're talking about gospel because we'd always put 'Just a Closer Walk with Thee' in every show. Even if we only did three or four songs, that was one of them. You could always hear a pin drop—even if we were performing in a hotel. There was a tremendous excitement and a lovely feeling.

So in 1964 you secure a gig with the Seekers as the musical entertainment on board the cruise ship Fairsky *on the way to the UK. You were only intending to go there for ten weeks and then return to Australia.*
That was the deal, yes. However, when we got over to England we were on television just about the first night. We were on at the Palladium within six weeks, and then we landed two television series as guest artists.

Take us through the roller coaster that it must have been as your music took off—and you still at a pretty tender age.
Oh yes, that's very true. It was amazing. It was a great variety of things we were doing. But luckily I was with the three guys and I think that made it much, much easier for me. I don't know whether I would have been able to do it on my own. It was just a whirlwind.

Of course, at the time you take it for granted. When you're young you think that this happens to everybody—all you have to do is turn up! It just seemed like it was all laid out for us. We had that uniqueness though—that's what made us stand out. We were very fresh faced, friendly, normal people. We weren't long-haired performers with electric instruments!

Can you give us a couple of snapshots of your most powerful memories—some of the great highs you experienced during that time?
Well, performing with the Queen Mother present was always wonderful. There was the huge crowd at the Myer Music Bowl,

200,000 people—that was wonderful. Becoming Australians of the Year in 1967 was absolutely amazing. Hitting number one with 'Georgy Girl'—to be the first Australian group to ever do that in the US. There are just so many highlights.

Did the four of you always get on?
Oh yes, always. We are still very good friends today too. I think the respect thing is a very big part of our relationship. We have a common sense of humour—we were always laughing. All the boys are very witty. A lot of it is nonsense, but it just bonds you together.

So you are now back on your first solo concert tour since 2001. What led you to jump back on the horse again?
The demand from the fans has been unrelenting. So many emails to my website—people are even coming from overseas. They've said, 'We'll go anywhere; wherever you're going to do the concert, we'll be there.' So I thought, 'I've just got to somehow do this and put one step on the stage and see how it goes.'

People have poured their hearts out to me. They tell me that the music I am making is meaningful for them and uplifting for them. I see it as a way of helping people. So it helps me because I have had enough experience now to know that if I can pluck up the courage and ask for the Lord's help, get up on stage and open my mouth—something is going to come out! I think the Lord is doing some trick! I'm serious!

Judith Durham's website allows you to hear samples of songs from all of her recent albums, including *The Australian Cities Suite, Gift of Song, The Hottest Band in Town Collection* and *Colours of My Life* <www.judithdurham.com>, <www.theseekers50th.com>.

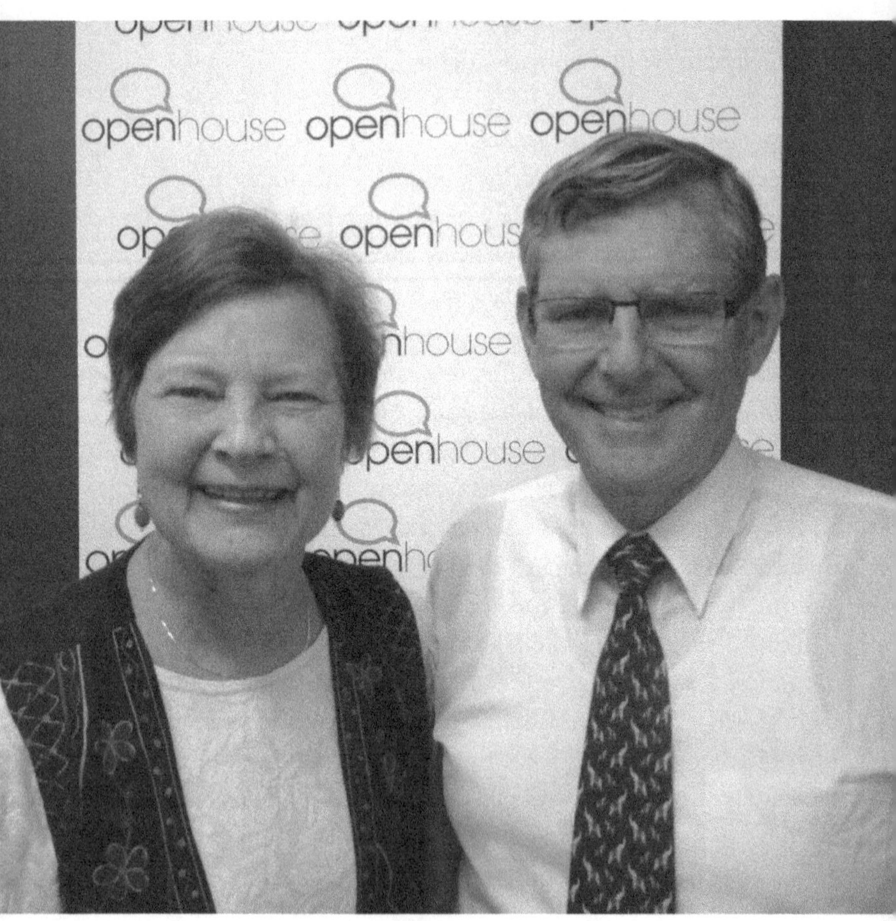
openhouse
openhouse
openhouse

Kay and Russell Clark

In the face of death

When someone stares death in the face from the framework of Christian faith, that framework has to be real—it has to be right.

Kay and Russell Clark have lived a rich and rollicking life, working in the world of medicine and a range of missionary posts. Those twin worlds have come together in a battle for life itself. Kay and Russell have been married for forty-two years.

Russell: I was a conscientious final-year medical student. I worked very hard and I was very serious. I didn't go out on Saturday nights to parties. My sister took pity on me. She said, 'I think you need a girlfriend and I know just the one for you. You'll meet her if you go to the Lake Macquarie Crusader Camp working bee.' So I set aside that weekend to go and meet this special woman that my sister had lined up for me.

It was a wonderful occasion. I met Kay there, but she wasn't the special woman. She was far too young, but she was clearly the best one there. I just made a mental note, 'I'll wait for this one to grow up.' She was sweet sixteen.

And you were?
I was a final year medical student—easily twenty-two. So I did the 'Christian thing'. I was the leader of a beach mission team and I invited her to consider joining the team.

Good move, Russell!
I could keep an eye on her there! I've been greatly blessed with forty-two years of marriage to this wonderful woman.

Russell, can you explain what you do for a job.
I am a specialist physician. I trained in Sydney at Royal Prince Alfred Hospital and I've run a department of medicine in Hong Kong. I started the geriatric department at St Vincent's Hospital where I was for seventeen years as a staff specialist. I was also a professor in an African medical school and the senior specialist in the Kilimanjaro Christian Medical Centre. I've now given up clinical practice but I continue teaching at the University of New South Wales Medical School and the Notre Dame Medical School.

Kay, at what stage did the penny drop that this mature young man had you in his sights?
I was interested in him, but he was very old and very kind of staid. I had to come to terms with that! It culminated on the beach on beach mission team night off. On New Year's Eve in the moonlight, the team leader went on his knees in the sand and proposed to me.

How romantic! So then began this rich and rollicking life. You ultimately went on to be missionaries. Russell, where did you go?
I was very greatly influenced when I was a boy by reading Paul

White's *Jungle Doctor* books. I believed that God was saying to me that I should do medicine and that I should be a missionary doctor.

No one in my family had been to university and no one in my family had anything to do with medicine and health issues. So it was really quite a big thing for a ten-year-old boy to get that idea. My parents were a bit anxious that I had tickets on myself to think that I could go to university and be a doctor. But I loved medicine once I got into it.

Africa was an option until I was a counsellor at a Billy Graham crusade in 1968. Billy Graham appealed to all the counsellors: 'Why are all you Christian people going off to Africa and India and not going to Indonesia? It's your neighbour and there's a great mission field there.'

To me that sounded like the right thing to do, so the focus was all on going to Indonesia. Then I thought, 'I need a wife—I can't possibly go by myself!' I wanted to give Kay the chance to think about whether she wanted me or not, based on the uncertainty of my future.

So what did you say, Kay?
I said yes straight away!

And no hesitation about the mission aspect?
That had already been one of the things on my radar. I'd done biochemistry, thinking that would be a good thing to use overseas.

Eventually it was Hong Kong you ended up in, and you spent ten years there with your family. Kay, tell us what that was like.
It was fabulous. It was a really exciting place to live, and interesting for our kids to grow up in a different culture. Not only was it

different racially but we lived in a very poor part of Hong Kong. The hospital was a Christian hospital, built to serve the people in the poor areas. It was very confronting for our kids to live among people who were very poor.

So you then came back to Australia, and in 1995, Kay, you suffered breast cancer, and it was pretty bad.
That's right—quite aggressive, fast growing. I thought I'd be dead in two years. I worked in breast cancer research at the time so I knew what to expect.

How did you manage that?
The right answer would be that I should have thought about what I needed to do. In fact, after about a year I worked out that I wasn't going to die just now; but it was a very good wake-up call to think about what matters in your life and what doesn't.

Some people would say it's a scary time, but I look back on it as a wonderful time because everything else pales into oblivion and your focus is on you and God. Lots of people were praying for me, obviously. I felt closer to God than I'd ever felt in my life before.

And you've no doubt been grateful for the years that followed.
I now think, 'Thank you, God. I've had a bonus of fifteen to seventeen years.' Back then I thought that was the end of our plan to work overseas again. I also thought I'd never have any grandchildren. Yet here I am now with eleven grandchildren and having worked for seven years in Tanzania.

Russell, what was it like for you to bridge those two extremes of being a professional and esteemed doctor and having this personal and fearful thing happening to Kay?

I often wonder whether it is good to be medically trained when your spouse has a medical condition. I think on balance it's better to know. Certainly for the next two years I was anxious. I took seriously the injunctions from the Scriptures to not be anxious but to pray, and I've never prayed as hard or as intensely. I prayed driving, I prayed whenever I wasn't doing something. I was bringing it before the Lord, and I felt that all would be well.

What worried me most, I have to say selfishly, was that I don't think I could have coped bringing up the children by myself. I feel genuinely very sorry for those people who get serious illnesses while they are still in the midst of childrearing. My heart goes out to them. We must care for those people more than anything else.

Eventually it came to me that I should pray that we would take it as a sign that if Kay was free of cancer within five years' time, we would apply to do mission work again.

Which you did, and ended up in Africa for another seven years of medical work. Kay, you took up some significant work there as well.

I was teaching in a Bible school which trained pastors for work in the churches—both men and women. They were the most appreciative students I have ever had. They were mostly older men and women with very little education. They had been to primary school. They put up with me teaching them in bad Swahili but they were so grateful for the opportunity to learn. It was wonderful—inspirational!

So after seven years in Africa, you'd been back for three years when your health, Kay, took another bad turn.
I'd had a minor slurring of my speech for about a year. I thought nothing much of it so we didn't do anything about it. Russell kept thinking what it might be and eventually we went to see a neurologist. I had some scans and they found I had a brain tumour in my brain stem.

How bad is that?
It will kill me. The statistics are that if it is untreated, you have three months survival; if it's treated, you have twelve months. It cannot be removed. It just grows and messes everything up.

Where are you at in terms of time?
Well, I think I'm in overtime already because I've had it for a year. That's one of the hard things. I like to be a bit in control and I have no idea how long I'm here for.

So it's an exercise of even greater faith at this stage?
Yes. I know where I'm headed. I know in whom I trust. It's part of my life.

How can you be sure of that?
Because God has promised and I've put my trust in him. Jesus says, 'I go to prepare a place for you', and I believe him.

Russell, what about you? How are you managing this time?
I'm much less anxious than I was last time. I really feel very much at peace about it all. I'm greatly encouraged because Kay reacts to this so positively and so well. It might be very different if she reacted differently.

We are very grateful for friends who are praying for us. It's something that we really wanted to let people know about. There are many people praying that Kay will be miraculously cured and that the tumour will go.

Kay: It won't!

Russell: It would be wonderful if it did. We would both be very grateful. But we are not counting on that at all. We are trusting that God will help us. We both thought that it was a bit easier at our age to get this diagnosis.

Kay: You have to get old sometime and die of something.

Are you fearful at all, Kay?
No, although I had a strange thing at one stage when I thought I was dying and I thought in the midst of it, 'This doesn't feel very pleasant. I don't like it!' I think Woody Allen said, 'I am not afraid of dying—I just don't want to be there when it happens.' No, I'm not fearful.

And there is certainly no denying it.
No, no. And I get impatient with people who say, 'Oh, I'm sure you will be healed.' I actually argue with them.

But it is an exercise of great faith—to have such trust.
God has never let me down. I can trust him in everything I have come across so far. Where else is there to go?

Russell?
I've been rehearsing over many years why I believe. Our existence can't be explained in any other way than a Creator God who has made us. I get increasingly angry and annoyed with the scientific community that thinks it has explanations of our existence. It is absolutely absurd. I can assure you, as a person trained in the biological medical sciences, that nothing can be explained other than [by the fact that] a great almighty being has brought us into being. I'm very sure of that. The more I study my medicine and teach my medical students, the more I reflect upon how we are truly designed.

I also reflect on what it means to be a Christian—it's knowing the presence of God with me day-by-day. The testimony of Job has always inspired me enormously: 'The Lord gives, the Lord takes away, blessed be the name of the Lord.' I've always thought, 'That's how I want to be.' I'm not pleased that my wife is going to die, but can I accept it? I believe so.

Kay, when this kills you—and I feel confident enough in you to be able to put it so directly—how would you like people to remember how you dealt with this?
Honestly. Openly. I figure I have nothing to lose, and to be able to talk about real things with people, to cut to the chase, is great. I guess that's the important thing.

To speak even hopefully, through faith?
Yes. I want to stop everyone and talk to them about it because it matters. Maybe they haven't thought about it. I'm thinking about it because obviously it is on my horizon. So I want other people to think about it too.

openhouse
openhouse
openhouse
openhouse

Lindy Chamberlain-Creighton

Forgiveness

Two of the most compelling interviews of our *Open House* year were with Lindy Chamberlain-Creighton and her former husband, Michael Chamberlain.

They became household names more than three decades ago after their nine-week-old daughter Azaria was taken by a dingo from their camping ground near Ayers Rock (now Uluru).

Michael has for the first time written his full account of this shocking, shameful episode of modern Australian history, and Lindy spoke to us movingly about forgiveness—and there's a great deal to forgive.

Not only did they have to deal with the death of their baby in such circumstances but also had to endure the suspicions and accusations of police, the Northern Territory government and the media.

Lindy ended up being sentenced to life in prison with hard labour, only to be released more than three years later.

In 2012, after four inquests, the Northern Territory coroner finally officially ruled that a dingo did indeed take young Azaria.

Lindy and Michael, separately, took us through their own personal journeys and anguish. Lindy began by painting a picture of her young family before that fateful trip to the Red Centre.

I had six-year-old and four-year-old boys. I was pregnant, keeping my fingers crossed that I was going to have a daughter at last.

And you had your girl, Azaria.
We did, we had a girl.

So the family took off for the long trip to Ayers Rock and then that memorable night. Can I ask you what first aroused your alarm?
Michael thought he'd heard her cry. I was sure she hadn't. I was sure Azaria was settled for the night. Then another camper, Sally Lowe, and our son Aidan both said they heard her cry. So I thought I would pacify them and go back and have a look. Then all hell broke loose.

Once the media got hold of this, one commentator wrote that 'your situation was a media dream. It had all the elements: mystery, instinctive fears, motherhood, femininity, family, religion, politics and tourism caught in forensic drama.' What do you think it was that drove the events that so comprehensively turned against you?
It's a little bit of everything.

Including human nature?
Human nature is at the bottom of everything, isn't it? Greed and selfishness make us do all sorts of things. As human beings we should be looking out for one another, but we seem to prefer to look out for ourselves.

How shocked were you to find yourself in the midst of what you called a 'fiasco' (and we need to keep on remembering that your nine-week-old child had just been killed)?
The thought that anybody had the audacity to accuse me of doing something to a child that I loved is just mind boggling. On the other hand, I've always had the personality that made me look at the facts and get on with them as quickly as possible. My dad taught me to always try and look at the other person's point of view.

However, it was very, very difficult for me to understand what had gone wrong. I knew the rangers were supportive and I knew the police were supportive. All of a sudden, though, those police disappeared and other police appeared with a totally different attitude. Yet they'd never been to the Rock. We'd never had any contact with them before, and all of a sudden they are trying to make me look guilty!

And yet as far as everyone saw on the TV each night, you both appeared calm, even serene about it all.
I wouldn't say that. If you look back at the raw footage you would see that neither of us was calm or serene or complacent about it. It was just fashionable at that stage to edit every time we got upset. My friends would say to me, 'You'd been crying before that interview—we could tell by your eyes.' The media would say, 'Well look, she's a hard-faced bitch—she's not affected.'

It was in the early days of when Rupert Murdoch had just taken over a lot of the press. In order to keep people watching the news, there'd be 'swing news'—make you look innocent one day and guilty the next. People began to watch the news as a kind of serial.

And if they put the name 'Lindy' on the front page, they'd sell more papers or magazines.
Yes. They used to tell me if my name was on the front they had to print triple as a minimum.

So how were you both coping in reality?
I was going second by second. That's where support is very important. The support we had from my parents and our lawyer Stewart Tipple was phenomenal.

And a lot of other Australians.
There was a huge number of people. When I was in prison I can remember times when I could literally feel the prayer surrounding me. It was almost like I was being wrapped in blankets.

How deeply did you dig into your faith as this frenzy took on a life of its own?
When I first looked into the tent, I knew in that split second that I had to have God. I couldn't handle it or go through with it. I had to have something other than myself.

Was there ever a cry to God, 'What are you doing?' or 'What are you allowing to happen in my life?'
Not really. I remember saying [to God] once, 'I don't know why this has happened. I don't understand whether I need to learn something or whether somebody else needs to learn something. I know one day you'll show me the reason, but in the meantime as long as you're with me I can go through this.'

I also remember praying just before the verdict came down at the trial. Instead of 'let me go home to the kids', it was, 'Well, Lord, you know better than me, so your will be done.' Then they knocked on the door and said the jury was back. I just knew I wasn't going home. But I was at peace with it because I'd said to God, 'I'll go if you babysit the kids.'

On that night when the jail doors closed behind you, can you describe what I imagine was the rollercoaster of emotions you were feeling?

Look, I was so flat by then, I was just absolutely drained physically. I was so tired I could hardly keep awake. I was just thinking, 'I can't handle this.' I was worrying more about what the boys were going to be told.

When I went to pray there was a big blank hole. In the end I said, 'You pray for me, God: I can't do this.' I felt so peaceful, and the next thing I knew it was morning—I'd had a good sleep.

I woke up and felt like somebody was looking at me. I looked out my window and outside the fence there was a dingo. I thought, 'You wretch, you're out there and I'm in here. I bet the devil put you right there to discourage me. Well, he's not going to do it.' I knew that whatever happened, at the end it was in God's hands. I always had the feeling that there was an end to it all—that I wasn't going to be there for life.

You went in with hard labour. I've always wondered what that amounted to.

Anything they asked you to do. Some of it was just petty stupidity and other stuff was hard. We had whipper-snippers which we could have used to do all the edges, but that was too quick. They got us blunt scissors to cut the edges with instead. That really used to give us blisters, sitting in the sun for hours. Then we did a storm drain with big rocks and cement, but we didn't have any cement trowels or work gloves. We just had to do it with our bare hands. We also scrubbed down toilets that had had drunk officers in the night before. One particular time I was given a toothbrush to scrub everything out with, so it took hours. Then I was yelled at because it took too long!

You went into jail pregnant with Kahlia and gave birth in custody.
Yes, and then got out for five months because (to quote one of them), 'That's just so you can put the kid somewhere.'

You and Michael divorced in 1991 five years after your release from jail, but your marriage had been unravelling for quite some time, hadn't it?
Yes. I think the case held us together a lot longer. I had been hoping it would fix some of our problems and that we could put it behind us and go on. However, it actually exacerbated them.

I remember Kahlia saying, 'I was so angry when you and Dad split. All I wanted was for you to get back together.' Then quite some time later she said that once it had happened she realised that both of us were so much happier apart and so was she.

And the next year after your divorce you met Rick on a speaking tour of the US. He'd obviously known about your life here.
I'd been speaking over there the year before and the divorce was going through. We met the next year. He had signed petitions in the US in the '80s. Friends have now said to us, 'We gave it a year

or two at the most.' We've been married twenty years last year and we're going stronger than ever.

One of the most powerful and probably, for many, puzzling aspects of your whole story is how you've been able to forgive everybody—the lawyers, the media, the police and the Northern Territory government.

That's easy when you realise what forgiveness is and how to go about it. Most people think forgiveness is for the other guy. It isn't for the other guy. Forgiveness is actually very selfish—it's you telling yourself, 'I don't have to bear their responsibility. I don't have to be responsible for the nasty things they have done. I don't have to be responsible for their punishment. That's theirs. I can hand all that hurt and nastiness back to them and get that right out of my life.'

Then I can take back my mind and not allow myself to be screwed up by it all. I can give myself permission to move forwards. It's all right to go ahead. I am not giving them permission to do this again. I am not saying that what they said is all right. I'm choosing to move forwards. I'm handing it all back to them, and now they're responsible for it.

Now if they want to deal with it in their life and realise that they are wrong and need forgiveness for it, then it's up to them to go to the person and say, 'I was wrong.' Then I'm very happy to say, 'Well, I've forgiven it, I've moved on—it's OK. Now you just work it out between you and God.'

It can be a tough thing to do, though.

It can be a tough thing to do, and sometimes I just think, 'I'd actually like to give you a smack!' I've often said in my talks that God is far more inventive in his punishments than I could ever be!

We are all responsible for our choices and decisions, good and bad. One day we will have to answer to him. He's the ultimate judge. If you consistently decided to hold a grudge, it's just like inviting somebody who hates you to come live in your house. They are living in your head. But by forgiving you take your head back and say, 'This is mine—you will leave!'

If anyone can know the reality of that, it is you, Lindy Chamberlain-Creighton. In 2012 the Northern Territory coroner at last officially declared that Azaria had been taken by a dingo, and in one very powerful moment in the court the coroner said she was 'so sorry for your loss'. What was that moment like for you?

I just thought to myself, 'You've had a loss too somewhere not too far away.' I knew she meant that. I could feel the fact that she understood. It was probably as important for me as the verdict. It's also the reason why I refuse to ask the Northern Territory for any apology. If you force an apology you know it doesn't mean a thing. When it is given voluntarily, as she gave hers, then it means something.

Are you hopeful for an apology?

I don't give it much thought at all. It's like the apology to the Aboriginal people: I'll be dead and gone before it happens!

But it would be nice, wouldn't it?

Look, there are still those who say, 'I know all about the lack of evidence, but I know things and I know she's guilty.' I'd be very happy if they did apologise, but I'm not going to hold my breath.

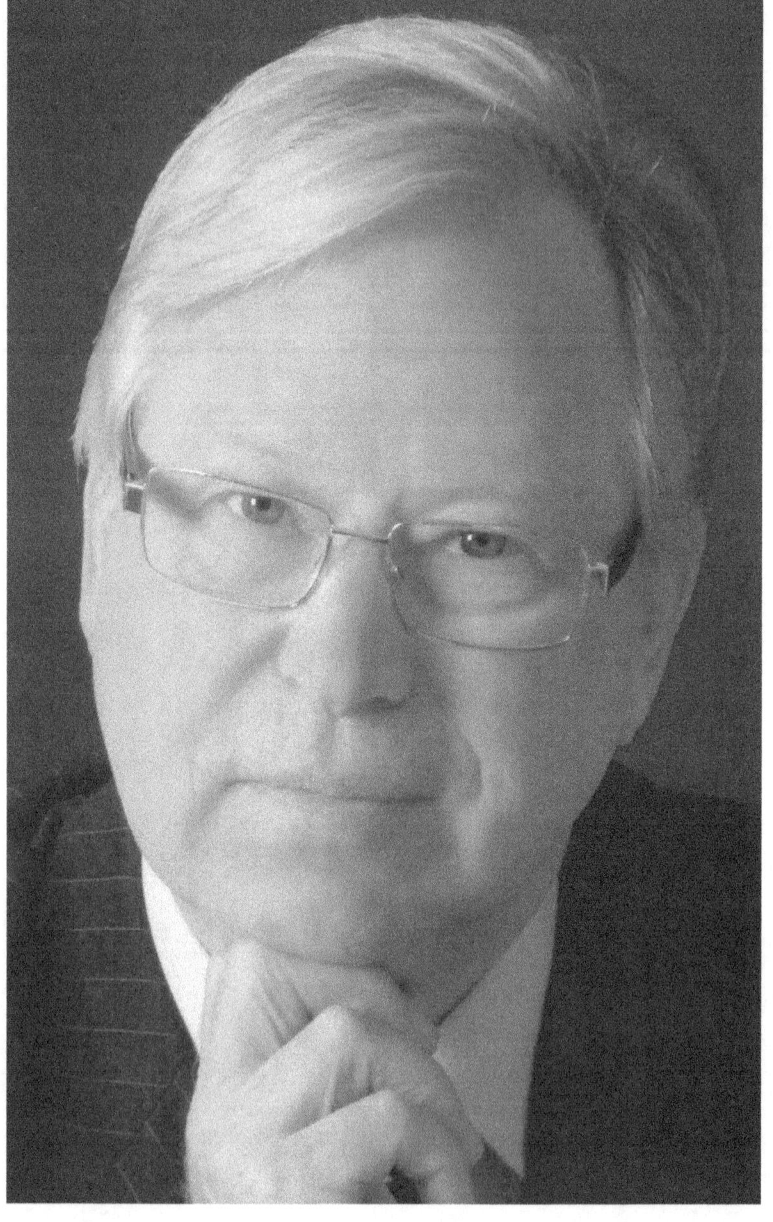

Michael Chamberlain

FATHER OF AZARIA CHAMBERLAIN

Michael Chamberlain took thirty-two years to finally tell the full agonising story of his experiences over the death of his young daughter Azaria.

As I read the account in his 2012 book *Heart of Stone*, over and over again I kept on thinking, 'What would it be like if this was happening to me?'

So much of the shocking abuse and injustice that he and his wife Lindy suffered stemmed from the perception, as Michael now describes it, that he was a 'religious nut case and a goof'.

So why did he feel it necessary to write his account more than three decades on?

That's a very good question. From the third inquest in 1995 something had snapped inside me, and a fairly high-up judicial officer said to me, 'You will never get justice in the Northern Territory, so don't start having another crack at it.' I said to myself, 'This is going to be a long haul', so I started to skill myself as a writer and researcher.

Has it been a good thing for you to write the book?
It has been an excellent thing for me to write and I feel really empowered by it. I was very fortunate that I had become a professional archivist. From day one I had written diary accounts, and I had collected newspaper [accounts], formal documents and all the court transcripts.

You say the book is about getting justice for Azaria. However, I kept thinking as I read your book: is justice ever possible for you and Lindy?
That is another very perceptive question. Justice in an imperfect world will only ever be imperfectly presented to you, if you're lucky and if you're alive still to see it. I guess that I am very fortunate that I was alive to see the day where the truth about how my daughter died was told in a coroner's court, and a Northern Territory one at that. But I have never had an apology from the Northern Territory government and that might take a little longer. I think my family, the witnesses and all the people in Australia, including Christians who supported us, deserve an apology.

Michael, can you paint us a picture of your young family and your lives together as you set off for that camping holiday to Ayers Rock from Mount Isa, where at the time you were a Seventh Day Adventist pastor?
Well, this is all very emotional still. The trip to Ayers Rock was quite a tough little trip in a smallish car. When we got to the Rock we were entirely overwhelmed. We saw a sign that said 'Do Not Feed the Dingoes', but that was about it. There was no warning at all about the trouble that dingoes were causing tourists. So we paid our $4 each and we put our humble little tent up—never suspecting for one minute that we would have any problems. What we didn't

know was that a week before a dingo had attacked a kid, almost in the same place where our tent was.

And on that night, August 17, 1980, you were the one who heard that now infamous cry.

Yes, the infamous cry from Azaria. It was urgent—it wasn't loud but it was a worrying cry, and I looked at Lindy and said, 'You'd better go and attend to Azaria.' The next thing she saw was a dingo coming out of the tent, head down, shaking. Lindy didn't see the child in the dingo's mouth, but it was heavy shadow. She said, 'Get out!' and then went into the tent quickly. She looked around in the rather dull, ambient light but couldn't see Azaria because the bassinet was turned on its side. But it didn't take long for her to scream out, 'That dingo's got my baby!' That was the horror sound which must have reverberated all around Ayers Rock on that cold clear night.

It was only a matter of seconds. We all tore out of the tent, but it was dark outside and my torch's battery had been flattened that day. If you've ever been to Ayers Rock and the desert surrounding it, it just all feels the same and it feels very, very threatening at night—no light. It all felt very hopeless early in the piece. How could this happen?

There were prayers said throughout that night as well.

Yes, there were, and I uttered one of them, as many others did. I have been rather badly judged on how I behaved in a religious sense there. I feel to this day perfectly justified in how I conducted myself, but that was misread badly. I think it was partly because of my Christian joy and the fact that I was Seventh Day Adventist. People tried to put the darkest interpretation they could on it.

You were widely judged, both you and Lindy, because of your calm outward demeanour. You didn't act like the public, the media or the police expected.
Yes, exactly.

So why did you appear like that?
Because I am a minister of religion. I am a Christian first and a minister of religion second, and peace and serenity pervade my soul. Graciousness pervades my soul. It pervaded my soul more back in those days—I'm afraid I've lost a bit of it now!

That's hardly surprising!
At the time, as a leader in your own church, as a person who ministers to others, you must hold things together. I was in seething turmoil inside but was just trying to keep a lid on myself.

So what was going on behind the scenes? There is public serenity, but what about away from the public?
Despair. Confusion. Terrible dread. And the loss of a child of ours—we were now going back to Mount Isa with one of our kids missing, and in a horrible situation.

How were you and Lindy at the time?
We couldn't talk about it. The trip back was really sombre. We got back to Mount Isa full of dread. We were met by very empathetic people, including members of our church, but within days people were starting to question.

This is the Northern Territory, the police and the media?
It was the police telling the media. My view is that somebody

was behind the police telling them, 'This cannot be—we have to have another story.' Tourism was becoming a new means of very significant income for the Northern Territory. The tourism consequences if it was known that a dingo had killed a child could be quite drastic, particularly for overseas tourists who had families.

Michael, are there words to describe what it was like to be at the centre of the media storm that you and Lindy endured over so many years?

While we were seen as pariahs and guilty people, it was horrendous. Every time I heard a helicopter I thought they were looking for me. Any time the phone rang I thought, 'Is this the media?' and it sent horror and a shiver through my spine. They were trying to paint a picture of us being the nastiest, most reviled people in Australia. I had no way, apart from my religious faith, of seeing any hope of it being changed.

And it was seen as 'crack-pot' religion.

Exactly. The fact that we were Seventh Day Adventists—there was extreme religious discrimination.

How did you endure that for so long?

Look, it's a very simple answer. My hope and my life and my gratefulness are all based on the fact that Jesus Christ died for me. He paid the price, and despite my infirmity, despite the fact that I am an imperfect person, he covers me. His life covers me and I am safe in him, regardless of whatever happens to me on this earth.

The second thing was that I knew I was innocent. I knew I was right and that I had to go on for my family and for all those now who were coming out of the woodwork to support us.

You were asked at the trial whether Lindy had cut Azaria's clothes to kill her and you replied, 'I don't think so.' Why did you answer it in that way?
That is a very good question. I said that because I have a very literal knowledge of what the truth is, legally and theologically. Ultimately—and I was too theological and probably too clinical for my own good—nobody knows anything unless first of all they are there, and then they have to believe that their eyesight is telling the truth. I was not there to see my wife do anything to the clothing.

So if they then ask me, 'How do you know that she didn't cut the clothing?' I have to say, 'Well, I *don't* know.'

Michael, on October 19, 1982, Lindy is found guilty of murder, a couple of years after Azaria disappeared. She's sentenced to life in jail with hard labour and you are found to be an accessory. Can you take us to that moment when the verdict is announced?
I was stunned. I had not seen it coming. Our own defence had said, after the summing up by the trial judge, 'No jury in its right mind could bring down a guilty verdict.' I could not believe I had been declared guilty when I thought it was an undeniably weak and circumstantial case against us, once you broke through the forensic rubbish that was being presented.

And Lindy waves what you describe as a 'haunting' wave to you.
She did. It was horrible because now she had life imprisonment, no parole, with hard labour. And this is the Northern Territory I'm talking about, 5000 kilometres away [from where we were living].

In jail, Lindy suggests to you actually ending your marriage. Yet she remains confident that God is in control and she will be released.
I think that's inevitable if a person thinks they are locked up for life. Lindy had been unhappy with my way of presenting evidence. She felt I could have been a lot stronger in defending her. One of my defence lawyers swore at me for it. It has become something that I have to live with. I don't resile from that. I did the best I could at the time. I was in a state of shock.

What did you notice about how Lindy had been inevitably changed?
She became more assertive and independent. That happens when you're alone. If you separate husbands and wives over a period of time, a wife, generally speaking, will say, 'Well, there's nobody around here to be my carer, my protector, my number one person. I have to do this myself.' This turns you into someone who becomes even more independent just to survive. You can't judge this as being right or wrong—it's just something that happens.

Fast forward to the coroner's ruling in June 2012. Are there words that you can use to describe that moment when the coroner handed down that ruling and also apologised to you?
Overwhelmed. Everybody in that court room was overwhelmed with emotion. First of all because of the just finding she brought down, and secondly because of the humane way in which she brought it down and the empathy that she herself showed. She was clearly affected by something that happened to us thirty-two years before.

Was there much said between you and Lindy on that day?
No, nothing much has ever been said since our divorce, nothing much at all. This whole case, since our divorce, was run independently. I never discuss anything with her. I ran my case myself and she ran hers. It was remarkable how aligned our cases were.

Michael, many years ago you left frontline pastoral ministry. You've re-married and your links to the Seventh Day Adventist Church remain.
Yes, they do. I'm still on the books as a church member. I don't attend church that regularly but I still have a great interest in the church's affairs, possibly from a distance.

Their support has been very significant.
Yes. Generally speaking, I can't fault the people in the Seventh Day Adventist Church for the way they have rallied around. The Adventist community is a great community to belong to. I have been involved in a Methodist community too, and they were wonderful also. But I can't fault the way Adventists rally around people. By lifestyle they are a very caring people. Of course, to have been so badly dudded by the rubbish that surrounded us was very, very offensive to Adventists generally. They have become even more shy of certain media methodology and the way they print lies.

Can I ask you about two emotions, Michael: anger and bitterness. Two emotions that I think, humanly, would be entirely understandable for all that you have been through.
I would hope that the graciousness that has been given to me to live my life through Jesus Christ would help me never to be bitter. But that does not stop me from being angry and righteously indignant about injustice and religious discrimination.

Three fundamental things which Jesus critiqued the Jews about were that they lacked justice, they lacked mercy and they lacked having a proper faith.

I tried to apply those principles and I think they stood by me very well. They stopped me from going over the edge. They prevented me moving from being righteously indignant and angry about injustice into the Dead Sea fruit of bitterness. Bitterness destroys you; righteous indignation empowers you.

Michael, how do you say, then, that you've been able to make it through all this?

First of all, knowing that I was right and that I was innocent of the taunts, the barbs and the lies that were told. The second thing is that I have been bought with a price. I am not my own, and I identify now with the one who made me and died for me and who will ultimately save me if I remain faithful. I can do no other; I can only stand on that. And for that I will be eternally grateful.

Michael's book, *Heart of Stone: Justice for Azaria,* is published by New Holland Publishers.

Rebecca St James

SINGER, AUTHOR, ACTRESS

Rebecca St James joined us on *Open House* as she was celebrating her first year of marriage. She was no ordinary bride and no ordinary woman.

Rebecca has an enormous global following with her prolific output of music. She's a Grammy Award winner.

Rebecca has also been a very prominent voice for purity in dating relationships, and around the same time she walked down the aisle to marry Jacob Fink, she put out her ninth book, entitled *What Is He Thinking?* Yes, a woman writing about what blokes are thinking!

Rebecca St James was born in Australia and has called the USA home for the past twenty years. So after her latest book and her first year of marriage, we asked her whether there were new things she had learnt about 'what he is thinking'—and what men are really like.

Absolutely! When you get married it's a whole new world! However, I do feel that I was somewhat equipped to understand guys. I'm the eldest of seven kids with five younger brothers. That definitely helped the transition to marriage.

It's very different when you have dated guys to then be married. I'd developed a pattern in dating of not wanting to ask for what I needed because I didn't want to be a 'needy girlfriend'. In marriage, I'm learning to ask for my legitimate needs as a wife and not to expect him to read my mind!

The biggest thing that has been helpful for us to learn, even while we were engaged, is not to let the sun go down without talking issues through. We did premarital counselling, which was amazing. I encourage every engaged couple to do that. Things came up in premarital counselling that were so wonderful for us to talk through. So we now have this pattern of making sure that if issues come up, we talk them through.

In marriage, honestly, we have had to have some tough discussions every now and again. We are closer on the other side of it because we are both committed to complete honesty with each other.

One issue that affects so many of us, married or not, is the busyness of life. You both have very busy, high profile lives, yours especially. How have you maintained a sense of connection between you in the midst of it all?

We really prioritise being together. My husband travels for work as well. I'm on the road doing a few shows so I'll meet up with him while he's travelling as well. We have definitely worked up a lot of frequent flyer miles and put in the hard yards to make sure we are together most of the time.

When we are both working, we prioritise time to get away from everybody and everything. Sometimes even go on a bike ride or walk and just be with each other—'us time' is a real priority. That definitely helps a lot in the busyness of everything.

How have you kept your spiritual connection both with each other and with God amid all those distractions and pressures, and in a new marriage?
One of the things that was really beautiful about our lead-up to marriage was that we were given a devotional book that Dr James Dobson from Focus on the Family had written with his wife Shirley. My husband, literally the day after our wedding, opened it up and led us in a devotion. That has been a daily thing for us. Even when we are away from each other, we will email the answer to the question of the day. It's an incredible connection for us, and prayer is a strong focus for us as well.

One thing I know you've been so pleased about is that your marriage ended your season of 'dating', in which you have taken a particular interest. Was that a pretty lonely time for you?
Yes. I'm so glad to say good riddance to dating! No matter how you slice the cake, it's a vulnerable season in your life.

I really wanted to pursue a book like *What Is He Thinking?* before I met my husband. I wanted to learn about men and dating, to encourage girls that there are good guys out there who have honourable intentions and who really want to live out relationships in God's way. I was dating Jacob when I was finishing writing the book, which was very unique, perfect timing.

Having the platform I had was a hindrance to my dating life. I know that for sure with a few guys I went out with. They were up front about the fact that my profile made them more insecure in our relationship. I think it's a difficult season in your life, and it was a long and lonely one for me—but worth the wait! I now see that God has redeemed my pain. He did not waste those years.

You've been a very prominent voice urging women to wait for marriage before leaping into sex. I'm starting to blush asking this, but was it worth the wait?
Oh my goodness, I'm so grateful every single day that I waited for my husband and that he waited for me. We exchanged purity rings in our ceremony, which was just such a beautiful example of faithfulness before marriage to each other.

I think a really big part of the blessing, unity, intimacy and closeness we sense is because we did remain faithful to each other before marriage. Whenever I talk about purity, I also talk about forgiveness. Many people have regrets in this area of their lives, so I always talk about the fact that God forgives and sets you free from the past.

What would you say to dating couples about waiting now that you have crossed that threshold into marriage and the waiting is over for you?
Apart from it being absolutely worth it, I would just say: put boundaries in place as a couple. Talk about boundaries. Protect yourselves from going down a path that makes it all about the physical. A marriage relationship is about every single part of you being united with someone else. It's not just the physical—it's the emotional and the spiritual.

I now see that for all my single years, I was a bride preparing for my groom. So that's what I am now saying to girls, and even to guys as well. Every decision you make will either bless your marriage or hurt it.

We live in a culture that thinks very expediently and just thinks about 'now'. If we started thinking about the future by living God's way in our single years, marriages in our culture would be much stronger.

In your book What Is He Thinking? *what were the things that men told you in your wide range of interviews that actually surprised you about them and how they relate to women?*
I think one of the things that stood out was one of the guys who said, 'If I'm dating a hot girl who is boring, it's an absolute turn-off for me.' He doesn't want just the outside appearance. He wants the heart to be interesting as well.

I thought that was a really great comment. So much of our culture just makes it all about appearances, but it's about the whole person. That's what these guys were saying over and over again. They were also saying that modesty is important, which again is something you don't hear in our culture. They were talking about wanting to honour God with the person they are dating in every way—to pursue him, pray together and have a focus on God in the relationship.

Near the top of the list of what men don't like is that they don't like critical women.
I think that was one of the most interesting parts of the book. I kept hearing from guys what a major turn off it is. A 'critical spirit' was top of the list, and that matches the biblical concept of not being a nagging wife.

Another thing that definitely came up was that guys are a little unsure now of their role when it comes to women. All of the guys were pretty traditional in that they wanted to be the one to ask a girl out. They didn't really want a girl to be asking them out. They wanted to be the initiators. I think every girl, if she really looks deep, deep into her heart, wants to be pursued, not to be the pursuer.

I know for me I would get upset that these guys were interested in me, yet they would not ask me out. They couldn't just step up and be strong. Knowing what I know now because of the research for the book, I would have had a little bit more grace with some of those guys. I realise that the model has changed. Dating has become more of a friendship-based model.

Another huge factor at work in much of this is body image. It's such a huge issue for young women. What do you say to them, out of your observations and experience, to help them with body image, self-esteem and ultimately their health?

I think we need to pursue healthiness in eating right, exercising and things like that. But I think too many of us, myself included, have made body image too much of a focus in our lives. If I felt like I was not in perfect shape, I felt so much shame. I have looked in the mirror at certain points in my life and apologised to myself with tears for being so critical. I was so hard on myself, so judgmental, and placing too much of my self-worth on how I look.

Guys can sense when we make it all about our appearance because then we are not free as people. Over and over again these guys are saying, 'We want a girl who is free, secure and knows who she is in God and is comfortable in her own skin—not obsessed about how she looks.' So I think that balance for pursuing healthiness in eating and exercise is a good balance to keep.

You are such a prominent and public figure with your Christian faith. Can I ask you whether that ever allows you to have private doubts or questions about it all? I read a tweet of yours the other day that said, 'Faith wouldn't be faith without having to trust what is unseen.'

I've struggled at certain points with feeling very public, especially when I was younger. I've often wondered what is actually mine and private and what belongs to everyone else.

I think all of us have moments at certain points of going, 'Man, I really don't understand that about you, God—that really is confusing to me and makes me question you.' However, underlying even the most painful and difficult times of my life was knowing that God was with me and that he is real and he is going to take care of me.

openhouse
openhouse

June Dally-Watkins

DEPORTMENT AND STYLE QUEEN

The life story of June Dally-Watkins is a truly epic, classic Aussie story. She went from small town country Australia to being swept off her feet by Hollywood heart-throb Gregory Peck.

For more than sixty years June has uniquely influenced hundreds of thousands of young Australians, and she remains proud to be a 'bushie' at heart. But for most of her outwardly glamorous life she has hidden a deeply painful side. It is an entire world away from her confident and successful public persona.

She attributes her enormous success and influence in Australia and beyond as a pioneer in etiquette and deportment to two simple things: love and care, the two foundational elements of her relatively recent but deep Christian faith.

If you don't have love and don't love yourself and care for yourself, I think you will be very empty and very unhappy. I believe that all human beings should love and care for the person who lives inside them. That will help them to give love and care to other human beings.

And it works.
Yes, it does. It does work. And after sixty-two-and-a-half years I'm still doing it!

June, can I take you back to Watsons Creek in northern New South Wales where you were born and grew up. Your mother was an enormously influential woman in your life.
My mother had to stay at Watsons Creek to care for me until I was old enough for her to leave with me. She always wanted me to be the best that I could be. She'd say, 'June, if you don't present yourself well in life, you won't be successful in life.'

Why do you think she wanted you to be so successful?
Because she'd had a very lonely, sad life. She gave up her life for me and stayed in this funny little deserted mining village called Watsons Creek. She stayed with my grandparents, where she helped run the property and cook for them. She was very beautiful and a delightful lady, but she had missed out on her opportunity in life and she didn't want that to happen to me. She wanted me to make up for what she had lost.

Your grandfather set the lead for manners and etiquette.
My grandfather was a wonderful man. I loved him. He was always strict with me. He always wanted me to write well, to read well and to study. He was always so gracious. He was a tin miner and then he was allotted some land and he turned that into a sheep farm.

June, your first introduction to the world of glamour that defined your life came in a mail order catalogue at the Watsons Creek post office.
Yes! I had to walk about three kilometres to the post office. I picked

up the mail order catalogue for Farmers Department Store in Sydney, where there were models even way back then. I wanted to be one of them! I would copy the poses of the models, light the candle in front of the mirror and copy them.

Then the *Women's Weekly* started to come and I read about movie stars and Hollywood. I would go out at night and look at the millions of stars up there at Watsons Creek and think, 'I wonder on which star is Hollywood? How would I ever get there?' I was dumb! In fact I heard the school teachers say that to my mother one day: 'Junie will be a failure in life; she'll never make it. All she does is sit and look out the window all day and daydream.'

Well, that wasn't a bad thing after all!
No, daydreaming is wonderful.

Then you were 'discovered' simply walking down the street in Tamworth, weren't you?
One day we were walking down Peel Street in Tamworth and this gentleman came to my mother and said, 'I'm a photographer and I'd love to take photographs of your daughter. You should take her to Sydney. I think she would make a great model.' I was thirteen.

So your mother took you to Sydney, and your adventures there sound so wonderful, so innocent, maybe even naïve—yet brimming with ambition.
Yes. We had nothing—no money. My mother had a Singer sewing machine, so when we came down to Sydney we rented a little room at Kensington and she made clothes for people. That's when she took me to Farmers.

What did she say to the people at Farmers?
She did the talking because I wasn't bright enough. I didn't have the confidence. They looked at me and said, 'Oh well, would she like to model a hat for our catalogue tomorrow?' I thought of everyone in Watsons Creek seeing me! My mother was thinking of how much money I would make: ten shillings and six pence. That was a lot of money.

Within a very short time you were Model of the Year and Australia's most photographed model. What a dizzying ride that must have been!
My mother and I went up to Watsons Creek for Christmas, and we went to the post office when the newspaper arrived. And there was a photograph of Junie and it said, 'Voted Australia's most photographed model'!

Also at this time, your mum comes up with the idea of a school of deportment, Australia's first.
Yes, but she didn't want it to be just a charm school. It had to be real, not just 'charm', because that would be too shallow. When all my girlfriends were going out and having a good time and marrying rich young men, I was there putting together a program on personal development. It's still going sixty-two-and-a-half years later.

You and your mum were both very ambitious.
Oh, my mother was ambitious. She knew that she had to encourage me to do well in life, otherwise I might just be stuck back there in Watsons Creek the way she had been, with no life. She encouraged me to have a dream, to imagine, to look at those stars and to think of what might be.

June, at the age of twenty-five you embarked on Australia's first fashion show to the US. I wonder how a girl who was still not long out of Watsons Creek dealt with such a culture shock? Suddenly you were at Marilyn Monroe's birthday party!
The fashion show I took was a one-woman fashion show, just me. I would put on a dress and walk out in front of the audience and I would tell them about the dress. Then I went to Hollywood and I was invited to Marilyn Monroe's birthday.

At last you were seeing your 'stars'. Then to Rome and Gregory Peck, in what you're careful to say was a romance, not an affair.
Yes, it was a romance. I was a very naïve girl. I believed you had to have pride in yourself.

I met Greg on the set of the movie *Roman Holiday* and he very kindly invited me out. He told me he was going to show me Rome, and he did. He took me to dinner and was very charming. Then Audrey Hepburn finished filming her part and left Rome to make another movie. As you know, at the end of every movie they have a breakup dinner, so I was invited to sit in Audrey Hepburn's chair with William Wilder on one side and Gregory Peck on the other.

He invited you to go to Paris with him.
Greg said, 'Now that I've finished *Roman Holiday*, come with me to Paris.' I said, 'Thank you very much, but I really have to move on.' But we stayed friends. Gregory Peck was a delightful, charming, sincere gentleman.

You felt drawn back to Australia.
My mother had given up her life for me. I would not let her down, so I flew back to Australia.

And you met John Clifford, who you thought at the time was an Australian version of Gregory Peck, and married him.
I already had my school and lots of students, the first outside London and New York. I wanted to be part of a family for the first time in my life. One day I looked across this crowded room and saw John.

On my wedding day I remember my father-in-law patting me on the head, looking at John and smiling, 'Don't worry, son, as soon as the children start coming she'll want to give up her business.' I said to myself, 'No way! No way will I ever give up my business.'

In those days, Leigh, a woman's job was in the home. She was supposed to stay at home, have the children, look after the children, cook the meals, do the housework, while the husband went out and worked or had a good time.

In fact, you received angry, hostile calls from people complaining about your lack of care for the children and the fact that your husband wasn't having dinner prepared.
'Poor John! Why are you neglecting your husband, and why aren't you home looking after your poor starving children?' But there was food at home, and I employed a nurse and a housekeeper. Nobody starved! I did give my children a hard time and was insistent that they were well mannered—all the things my mother insisted upon. They used to object, but now I hear them telling my grandchildren exactly the same things.

So many years have gone by, June—more than sixty years of your school and 300,000 students. What has been your greatest desire for them as you've equipped them for life?
To feel happy in life; to be self-contented; to do well in life and

not waste their time. Wherever I go, ladies come up to me and say, 'Miss Dally, remember me? I did your course fifty or sixty years ago.' Students come up now and say, 'Miss Dally, my grandmother came to your school, and my mother.'

I want them to be self-confident—to feel good about themselves, to be able to cope with life anywhere in the world. My mother used to say: 'Junie, wherever you go in the world, you have to be acceptable.'

I wonder how much of all that came from one very painful part of your life that remained hidden for so long.
Leigh, no one ever talked to me about my father and I never brought the subject up.

Your mum was a single mum?
Absolutely, and that's why she had to stay at Watsons Creek with my grandparents so that I could be raised there. I often wondered who my father was. My mother never talked to me about him. It was never discussed by anybody. Major David Dally-Watkins adopted me when my mother married him and we came to Sydney to live.

From time to time, among the audience when I was doing the mannequin parades, I would be walking along the catwalk and I'd notice a particular man and think, 'There's that man again.' Many times he was there and I started to wonder who he was. When my mother died, I was teaching at my school and one of the teachers came in and said, 'Miss Dally, there is a man outside who wants to meet you.' I went out and as soon as I saw him I knew. He said, 'I'm your father, and now that your mother is no longer here, I want to look after you and take care of you.' Then I did get to know him, but I didn't like him.

That must have been such a challenging experience.
And hurtful, emotionally hurtful.

But, Leigh, the Lord has always played a part in my life. I used to think my grandfather was my guiding light. He was the one who looked after me when I was young. Then I realised that I was being guided apart from my grandfather. There was someone in my heart and soul—somebody was there who seemed to guide me.

It wasn't until the '80s that you started to see that light of Christian faith in your life, was it?
I had a school in Hong Kong. One day I was walking down a street and a woman I had known stopped me and she said, 'June! What are you doing in Hong Kong?' She was with Youth With A Mission. I'd known her as quite the party girl in Sydney! She said, 'Come and join us for our prayer meetings on Wednesday nights.' I did, and I became absolutely addicted. They took me over to Lantau Island and dunked me in the South China Sea and baptised me!

Why do you think you became so addicted to this Christian faith?
Whatever happens in my life, being a Christian and loving the Lord just gives me such comfort. I'm not alone any more. I also want to do something that is worthwhile. I met Malcolm and Sally from Crossroads* and travelled over to Bosnia and Herzegovina after the war there, twice, taking in relief goods. I remember the first time I raised quite a bit of money to take to the people in need over there. My family said, 'Nonna, you're so stupid to do that! You might be arrested for carrying that money with you!' I put it in a belt around my waist and took it to the people who

---

* Australians Malcolm and Sally Begbie are founders of the Hong Kong-based charity Crossroads Foundation <www.crossroads.org.hk>.

needed it. I've been a Crossroads ambassador for more than sixteen years now.

What a wonderful work. June, what do you say now about Jesus Christ? I just feel that he is part of my life. And real: I *feel* the Lord. I just feel Jesus. When these miracles happen, I know where it's coming from.

Everybody has miracles every day in their life but they don't always recognise them. I say to our students, 'You have to understand that there are three parts of the human being. There is our body, which is the house in which we live. You must carry it well and tall and straight, with confidence. There is our mind, which is our "control tower". It tells us what to do, tells us how to speak, makes our ears listen—it is in control of us. The third part is our soul, which gives love and accepts love. It's what keeps us in peace. All those beautiful things that you can't buy.'

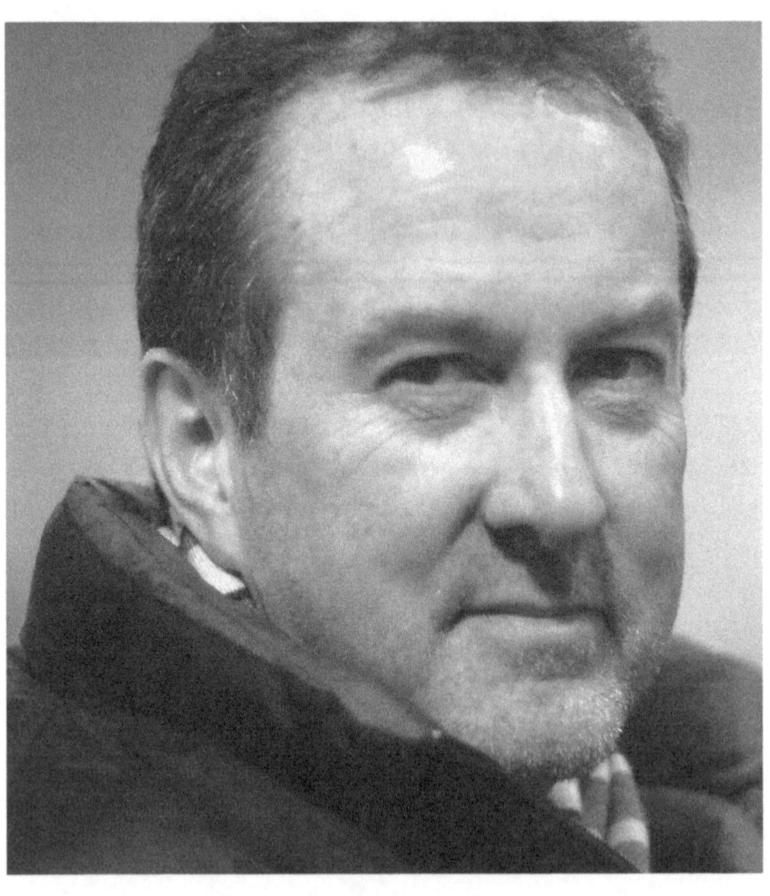

Ralph Winter

VETERAN HOLLYWOOD PRODUCER

Hollywood is home to the movies, fame and fortune—but is there a place for faith? Ralph Winter is a long-time, hugely successful Hollywood producer. His films have grossed an estimated $2 billion—all the way from *Star Trek* to *X-Men*. He and Australia's own Hugh Jackman have become close colleagues and friends.

Ralph brings to the big blockbusters he produces a sense of a bigger picture. We caught up with him in the midst of one of his movie shoots in Australia and got the obvious question out of the way first: what's Hugh Jackman really like?

He is a gentleman. He's fantastically talented, smart and engaging. For me what you see is what you get when you see him on television or in the movies. He is the real deal—that's what you see. He is a real artist and a great ambassador for Australia.

It's probably worth asking you to explain what a producer actually does. It's a familiar title, but people may not be familiar with the range of tasks it involves.
My wife is always asking me what I do, every day!

A lot of wives do that!

The credit of producer in the motion picture industry is very close to the title of director. It's actually the highest award given in the motion picture industry. The Oscar for 'Best Picture' goes to the producer. That's because a producer is someone or a group of people who has to pull it all together and drag it over the finish line. They have to be the leaders, the champions, the cheer leaders, the people who make it happen. They're where the buck stops.

How long will a typical big budget movie—for instance, X-men*—take to put together before even one frame of film is shot?*
The first thing is developing a great story. On the movie *X-men Origins: Wolverine*, which I shot here in Australia with Hugh, it probably took a year to develop the screenplay. Then I came down here in August of 2007 and we finished shooting in June 2008. The movie came out in 2009. So it's a two- to three-year process.

When you were assigned a movie to produce in Australia, what was your response?
I was thrilled! I made the decision very quickly, partly before my friend Hugh called me and said, 'Please come, please do this. I can't do it without you!' It doesn't take much to say yes to that. I love coming here. I love the people and love being in the city. I brought my wife down near the end of the shoot for a month and we had a great time.

Your business is very much a people business, isn't it?
Every business is a people business. If you want to break into investment banking you have to build relationships. You can't just jump into it. I think every business is that way, but yes, the

movie business is about relationships. If you're going to build a career you have to make friends along the way from the beginning to the end.

One of the things that is unique about the movie business is that the people who work for you on one movie, in a few years you could be working for them! So you have to maintain good relationships every step of the way.

I think there's also an added responsibility in dealing with people who have an impact on popular culture. Right or wrong, they have an impact.

Ralph, does a producer start his career watching a ridiculous number of movies?

I fell into this [career]. I am a history major and didn't really have any plans to be in the movie business. I was going to be either an academic or a teacher, or maybe even a pastor. I fell into making industrial videos for a company in Los Angeles, and they did well.

Then I had an opportunity to move to Paramount. I worked in post-production and then, yes, I began to watch a lot of movies and read screenplays. I began to appreciate what the business is all about and to learn. I worked hard on a lot of movies to gain some insight, knowledge and experience about how to make movies.

I think making short films is a great 'calling card'. The time working in making short films was my film school. I got to make fifty of those—that's how you learn.

What drew you to Hollywood—and why movies?

In movies there is an opportunity to tell a story in a deeper way. It's not necessarily the best way to make the most money. It's not necessarily the way to have a consistent career. But it is an opportunity to tell stories that go deeper, longer and further and can potentially have an impact.

A lot of people can remember the movies that moved them ten or twenty years ago—hero stories, journeys that resonate inside people. I've always been attracted to that. Movies are what I love.

In an age of such change in communication and entertainment, how are you struck by the enduring nature of movies?
They will not go away. Movies are the opportunity to be in a big room with spectacular sound and presentation, sharing it with a crowd of people. People around the world love going inside that dark room. I think that's just the current representation of what mankind has done around campfires for thousands of years.

And certainly telling stories is what Jesus did.
Jesus is an expert in telling stories. The Bible has five hundred or six hundred stories that are fantastic, with real, genuine, authentic characters, explaining what happens to them. These stories deal with real life and the solutions to life people find in their journey.

Ralph, can you tell me the three most significant work skills you bring to being a successful producer?
I think number one is being a leader. I get hired by the studios to provide leadership.

The second skill-set is managing expectations. There are so many different expectations—how much money should be spent and who should spend it, who to put into the movie, how the director will deliver the movie and what the studio wants. There are so many moving parts, and managing all those expectations is part of the job of a producer.

I think maybe the third thing would be how you deal with people relationally—respecting people, creating an environment where they can be creative and do their best.

And Christian faith can fit into that world?
I think if you are embracing your faith as a Christian you are necessarily thinking about relationships, and the process and the journey that everybody is on. How you treat people along the way is the best indicator of what you believe as a Christian.

I don't believe that the workplace is necessarily a place to proselytise or to try to convince people that the Christian faith is what they should embrace. The way you treat people along that journey speaks more loudly than words.

I feel like I have a base and a foundation that will withstand the rigors of making a movie—all the tension, all the struggles, all the obstacles, and the hard work that needs to go into that. I have a faith in God that I know will sustain me through that process.

What would you say working in Hollywood has done for your faith?
I have learned a great deal about how stories are made and told and the value of that. I think there is plenty we can learn and apply in the way Jesus tells stories and the way we as Christians should be telling the gospel story to a world that yearns for hope and a better way.

Because we have not done that as well as we might or could have?
Yes, that's primarily what I'm driving at. Unfortunately, we do not tell stories as well as Hollywood. With 'Christian movies' (whatever they are), it's like being a Christian plumber. I don't want a Christian plumber; I just want someone to fix my pipes! I don't want someone

to come pray over my pipes! I think that too often we come to the task of telling stories with an agenda. Too often Christian movies are answering questions that no one is asking.

The more we tell authentic stories and tell them in entertaining ways, the more there is an opportunity to get a fair hearing of what we believe in the marketplace.

Because it takes subtlety to draw people in.
It does take subtlety, but it also takes skill in storytelling. It takes the ability to tell a compelling story. Those stories in the Bible are compelling, but a lot of times as Christians we are so wanting to tell the answer that we end up not telling an authentic story—with all its grittiness, reality and the flawed natures of the characters. We always want to make it better. We want to tell a cleaner story. I think those stories are *less* attractive in the culture.

The skill and subtlety of telling a story well does not mean that you sell out on the message that the story is meant to deliver.
Right. I think you can tell the story of human struggle. You can show the struggle that Abraham or Moses or Samson or Elijah had, telling the real story. You don't have to talk about the answer or the message because it will come through. It will come through as the character shows you what they value and how they respond.

Can I end our wonderful conversation with one question about two elements of Ralph Winter: the single biggest highlight of your life and the single biggest highlight of your work?
I value my marriage. I've been married thirty-eight years. I've made choices along the way because of my wife. We have a great

partnership and marriage. It just gets better and better with our kids and our grandkids.

In my career a lot of people ask, 'What is your favourite movie?' My answer is, 'I love all my children.' I think the second X-men movie and the fourth Star Trek movie are certainly my favourites. I enjoy watching those movies and I enjoy how they've had an impact on the culture.

Peter Jensen

Former Anglican Archbishop of Sydney

Peter Jensen has had a significant impact on the arena of Christian faith in Australia, and indeed around the world. In 2013 he retired from the influential role of Anglican Archbishop of Sydney.

He's a man who often arouses great passions—both for and against. However, very much under the radar, far away from his public duties and profile, Peter Jensen has exercised a very important ministry. From the very early days in his role, he quietly, personally embarked on visits to a range of jails in which he met and spoke with prisoners and their chaplains.

When he joined us on *Open House*, his passion for this work was evident. It was also a chance to look back over twelve years in a challenging high-profile position.

When I became Archbishop, I knew that I couldn't do everything. I thought to myself, 'Who are the most dispossessed, the loneliest, the people in the most difficult situation in our community?' I came quickly to the view it was people in prison. I set about seeing if I could do things to help our prison population, and also to help us do better in this whole area as a society.

I've always been struck by the vision of Karl Barth, the great theologian, preaching in prison. I thought, 'If one of the greatest preachers and theologians in the world found himself there, it is the right place for the Christian faith to be.' In a sense that inspired me.

The thing that got to me was the whole idea of people no longer being their own master. It struck me that if we wanted to test a civilisation and how well it was doing, we would ask ourselves, 'What do we do with people in prison?'

Was it a confronting thing for you to first walk into that prison and have that door shut behind you?
Yes, of course. It is confronting when you see the actual conditions in which people are held. Let me say that in many ways I would rather be in prison in Australia than in other parts of the world. At some levels our society and our civilisation is doing well in this area—comparatively speaking.

However, there are too many people in jail. There are people in jail for too long who haven't been brought to court yet. There are too many people in jail from certain backgrounds and there are too many people in jail with mental health issues that are not being attended to. There are too many lockdowns in jail, where people are in their cells for too long. There is not enough being done for rehabilitation.

Let me also say I understand the situation because keeping people in jail is a very expensive undertaking. It costs maybe $70,000 a year to keep a person in jail, and the government doesn't have infinite cash to do all that it may want to do.

Were there things that you learnt about the human condition in being exposed to such a different area of life than you would have known before?

Yes. This is a strange thing to say perhaps, but in a way more spiritual work is done in prison. People are forced to confront who they are and have a great deal more time to think about it than in other places. It interested and surprised me that quite a number of the men and women I met were deeply reflective. They were responding to their situation by thinking though some big issues.

I also came to see just how important prison chaplains are and how much they are appreciated in their work. I believe that of all the things the state can do in regard to prisons, it needs to support prison chaplains—one of the key things, I believe, for the good of the whole system. I also had great respect for the prison officers I met. I thought a number of them were very thoughtful and committed to their role in ways which may have surprised you.

Is there one particular person's story that stands out for you as especially memorable?

There was a big man in one prison. His life story has been so grim that this particular person is kept away from all other prisoners. He has proven to be a danger to police and to others. I was able to meet and talk to this person and to recognise, in the light of what the chaplain told me, that even in the midst of his very difficult life there has come something of a healing touch from God. It is generally recognised by those around this person that a transformation has occurred. I can only stand in awe at what has happened.

This is the stuff of miracles.
It is the miraculous power of God's Holy Spirit. God did a miracle for me when he took me as a fifteen-year-old and brought me into his kingdom. It's a very big miracle for God to take a priggish, good works, goody school-prefect type and turn them into a Christian. That's a miracle, and I suppose it's just as big a miracle to take this man who had no chance in life and who had turned bitter and transform him. Praise God for it.

Looking back over your twelve years in this crucial and influential role, I'd like to ask you a few simple 'bullet point' questions. First one: the greatest surprise?
I've been watching archbishops for a long time and in one sense there was no surprise. However, I *was* surprised by one thing. If I may say so, you told me about it [before it happened]. I thought I had been a public figure because I was the principal of Moore College before I became archbishop. But becoming an archbishop turns you into a public person overnight. That's not something that any amount of training or life experience can prepare you for. It just happens, and you have to learn on the job. You told me that, you warned me—and it was helpful.

And it's rough.
And it's rough. That was a surprise. I just have to say to the man who succeeds me, 'You are in for a surprise, no matter how much you're prepared for it.'

What was the greatest challenge in this role over the last decade-plus?
I identified early on the greatest challenge facing us for the Christian faith in Australia is evangelism—sharing the gospel. Something like sixty per cent of people in Australia really don't know a full-on, Bible-based Christian person. How then can they hear the gospel of the Lord Jesus?

Therefore, I regard it as my greatest challenge to help Christians everywhere to share the gospel more broadly with people in our society. That continues to be the challenge. Since I live trusting in a God of hope, I have confidence that we'll do this.

There was the very considerable effort when you wanted to get ten per cent of Sydney people into a Bible-believing church. Why do you think that didn't happen?
First of all, I never thought it would. I always said that if such a thing happened, it would be a complete miracle and only God could do it. The idea of the ten per cent was to focus us not so much on growing our churches from within. We're not too bad at doing that, but we need to reach out. So the ten per cent goal was actually quite successful, because it forced us as Anglican Christians to start looking out into our community. Indeed, to a certain extent that has begun to happen. I am satisfied that we have begun that job.

On the other hand, I have to say that our churches have grown at about the same rate as the population. We've grown in the last decade something like seven per cent. That's good—I'm glad we didn't go backwards! It's tougher each decade. In the old days we used to be able to rely on a steady stream of English migrants to fill our churches. That's no longer the case. So to have grown seven per cent in a time when people are coming from all the nations of the world is not bad.

However, it's nowhere near where we need to be, so the challenge still lies before us.

There has also been an international dynamic that has marked your time in this role. I heard one historian speak of the rise and rise of the Sydney Anglican model of faith and ministry on the world stage.

Historians aren't always right, of course. They generally think about the past rather than the present. In fact, they are often wrong about the present!

By God's providence and the work of great ones in the past, the Sydney Anglican diocese has consistently taught the word of God, learnt the word of God and lived the word of God. Moore College has consistently stood for a learned, erudite biblical theology. It takes the brain seriously; it takes the heart seriously. It has been a launch pad for so many. Therefore, when the moment arrived for us to impact world Anglicanism, we were able to do that.

Interestingly, with the present great controversy about human sexuality, which started in America but now impacts world Anglicanism, it's been virtually the diocese of Sydney that has provided the biblical foundations to which so many in other parts of the world have looked. Of course, there have also been many other individuals and many other groups. Anglicans around the world are being reassured that they are not being foolish in their opposition to the liberalism which has so engulfed North America. We have played our part.

But, Leigh, here's an Australian thing to say: let's not exaggerate it. It's not that important. The Lord gives and the Lord takes away. While we may feel thankful to God that he allowed us to play a part, let's not think we played an indispensable part in what we did.

So that's the greatest challenge. What has been the greatest delight of this job?
It's a funny one—it's local churches. Christine and I have travelled around literally hundreds of our local churches. Going around and meeting with God's people in all the different parts of this diocese has been a great delight. I love Christian ministers and I love the work they do. I think they are undervalued because it's a tough job. Meeting them, talking to them and their wives and rejoicing in their children has been a great delight.

So, last bullet point question: one significant moment, through all of the significant moments I'm sure you have had in this job?
Of course, I've been present when someone has experienced 'new birth', becoming a Christian. It's like seeing a 'grace quake' occur. However, the first thing that comes into my mind is a different thing, and it's a bit selfish, I'm afraid.

I was at one of our churches a few months ago and a gentleman came to me and he said, 'You won't remember me, but I was the person who counselled you at the Billy Graham crusade in 1959.' I'm a bit of an emotional person, believe it or not, and I think I cried—inside anyway. I just thanked him.

I was also very conscious of the fact that here was a man who had been faithful to the Lord himself for all these years. It was as if the Lord had given me something very precious there.

The moment when I went forward at the Billy Graham crusade, accepted Christ and became a Christian is the greatest moment of my life.

I'd also want to say to everyone reading this: the greatest experience that any human being can have is to meet Jesus Christ and to receive him into their heart, and to live by faith in your Lord Jesus. And then to long to meet him at the end of life—to go to be with Jesus and to be like Jesus and to spend eternity with Jesus. That's what your future can be. So I would say to everyone: I hope you've done it, and if you haven't, let me urge you to receive Jesus.

Two final questions: one regret and one expectation for the future?
I look back and think of many missed opportunities, many things I might have done differently. In prisons, for example, I did want to do something, but there are many things that I didn't do. I didn't follow that through relentlessly enough. I also think I could have done better to inspire our churches and our people about evangelism. We have failed to inspire, to train and to set free our 'lay people'. That's been a weakness, but I'm hoping we will do that in the next step of our mission.

Is there one expectation for the future?
All I'm expecting is to continue what I do. I should have talked much more about Christine! As with most clergy ministry wives, she plays a part in ninety per cent of what I do. Christine and I have a special prayer—that the Lord will help us to find and do the good works that he has prepared for us this day.

As far as expectations are concerned, if we just keep praying that prayer, the Lord will open up opportunities for us to continue to serve him in the days ahead. That's what I'm hoping for. And then—I'm hoping to see Jesus.

Tony Hoang

FORMER GANG MEMBER, DRUG ADDICT AND DEALER

When you look into Tony Hoang's eyes you can see two lives—two compelling stories.

The first is the life of a fearsome member of a notorious Asian gang, a drug addict and a ruthless drug dealer. The second is a life totally transformed as a result of one seemingly 'chance' moment on a street at Cabramatta in Sydney's west.

Tony is the son of parents who were among Australia's first wave of 'boat people' fleeing the Vietnam War. Many would recognise his face from the compelling SBS documentary *Once upon a Time in Cabramatta*, which traced the struggles and crime in what was known as 'the heroin capital of Australia'. Tony was in the thick of it.

But his is also a story of rescue and redemption, and your spirits will be lifted to see where he is today.

My earliest memory would probably be of my father beating my mum. I remember a time when my mum came rushing into my room after my dad had beaten her, along with my sisters. I was about five or six years old. Coming home from school, all I would hear would be arguments and they often turned violent. A lot of the time the arguments were about money.

What impact does that have on a six-year-old, to see his dad beating up his mum?
Being the youngest and having six older sisters, for me he was my only role model and my reference point as a man. What every young man needs is a father figure or someone to look up to, but my role model was basically a violent man.

Obviously you're going to be very scared at a very young age.

Did you feel a sense of responsibility or guilt that you were the only male and this was happening and you couldn't do anything about it?
Yes. There was a combination of rage and the frustration of being so young and not being able to do anything. I felt a need of acceptance due to the rejection that I felt from my father. So that caused in me, as I look back now, a deep desire to be in the cool group, or accepted in a gang or a group of friends where I counted as somebody.

It was particularly difficult for the Vietnamese men to settle into Australia under the circumstances of that time, wasn't it?
Having been raised up here and educated here, I look back and try to put myself in my parents' shoes. My father didn't get that education. He didn't have those people skills. He didn't know how to communicate, especially coming over here with a different language. He resorted to alcohol, and that addiction carried on to me with my addictive personality.

Was there much help from Australia or Australians to settle families into such a radically new life?
I remember living in Bondi in a flat. There was an old lady who lived down the street who was very, very kind. I'm pretty sure she must have been a Christian. I was very young at the time, under five years old. All I remember are the Mars Bars she gave us!

You went to church as a young kid—what did that mean to you?
My parents were Catholics and very religious. *I* was very religious. I went through all the sacraments. I was an altar boy. I was brought up to believe in God, so I went to church every week without fail, even though I lived the life of a drug dealer and a gang member. Come Sunday I would go to church because I knew it was the right thing to do. I'd give my money and I'd do the sign of the cross.

I'd even go to confession. I wouldn't confess the crimes I did, so it didn't mean anything to me, even going every week. I wasn't living it. Yet I was the guy who would turn to his sisters to tell them to shut up during service, listen to the priest and show some respect.

I thought I was a good person. Even though I was making and doing all those bad things, I still thought in my heart of hearts that I was good person. Obviously you hold your head up high when you go to church every week.

Tony, tell me what those early days in the gang were like for you.
I was thirteen when I first started. I got drawn in by the thought of making quick money. Eventually I got caught up in all their fights. I missed out on my childhood where I should have been riding around on bicycles, going to corner stores and playing games. Instead I was driving cars around delivering drugs.

You had that sense of identity in the gang?
I did, and I guess that's what I was looking for. It was also good just sitting in a restaurant having your meals paid for—feeling important. It just felt good to have back-up if you fell into any trouble.

Why did the beatings and fights happen?
A lot of it was over money—people owing money for drug deals. Even if you looked at someone wrong you could get a beating. Even at the table, to point the teapot in a certain direction was a sign of disrespect, so you could get a beating for that.

Did you enjoy the beatings when you inflicted them?
It was an adrenalin rush, especially when it was my issue. I enjoyed revenge. Yes, I developed a bit of a taste for blood. By the end of it I knew it was wrong. Somewhere deep down in my belief system, I knew it was wrong.

Did you ever see someone killed?
One night I was in a club—there were about ten of us. Within minutes of walking inside the club, this guy pulls out a gun and shoots another guy right in front of me, about three to four meters away. The evacuation happens and we're all standing outside the club. All we could think about was that we wanted our money back—don't worry about this guy who is dying! I've seen things that I guess I should not have seen, things that I still think about now.

And drugs were an integral part of that gang?
Yes, more and more when the money started flowing through. Money just got hold of everyone.

And very quickly it all landed you in jail.
Yeah. At fourteen years old I landed in prison. I remember sitting in my cell thinking about my life. My only memory was dealing drugs and violence, so part of me couldn't wait to come back out. Another side of me wanted to get my life together and make my parents proud. So it was a bit of a struggle.

When I did come out, I was confronted with those two choices. That's where I made the dumb choice to continue on in that lifestyle of gangs I'd been introduced to at thirteen.

I came out and tried to go back to school. No school would accept me, so for the next seven years I dealt drugs. At the age of fifteen I moved out of home and got heavily involved in the trafficking of big quantities of drugs and dealing to dealers on the street. Anything I could get my hands on I would deal, and I would make $7000 to $10,000 a week at the age of sixteen.

And your own drug habit?
That came along with all that. I had a lot of money, I had a lot of things, but what came with that was a drug addiction. It started off with marijuana and then went on to heroin.

It only ever gets worse, doesn't it?
It does, it does, you know. I started injecting after four years, which really destroyed my life.

It took the lives of many of your friends as well.
Yes. I lost a very close friend at sixteen years of age. Another three would go in the next couple of years. By the age of twenty-one I'd already had three friends murdered and three who had overdosed.

Tony, paint me a picture of what each day was like at the depths of that drug habit.
It was a struggle waking up every morning, knowing that I had to rely on this product from hell just to make me feel normal. It was depressing. On the outside I painted myself as someone who had it together, who had a lot of money. But inside I was just torn apart, having no hope, having to rely on this drug day in, day out. It was ripping me apart.

Did you have a desire to get off it?
I did. Every addict does. But somehow it always gets the better of you.

You were still dealing at this time?
I was still dealing at the time, yes.

And big money?
Big money, although it got less and less as the years went on.

Because you were less and less functional?
Yes.

Did you come close to losing your life?
I have, many times. One time I was shot at inside a club. I was nineteen years old, and from point blank range this guy took two shots at me and somehow it did not get me. I witnessed a miracle right there!

Did you have enforcers?
I did. A lot of friends from high school, some of my sisters'

boyfriends at the time or other gang members. People knew of my family—they knew the amount of money I was making at that time and the connections I had. I did my own thing.

Then there came a time, at the depths of your drug habit, when you cried out to God.

Yes, I did. I had faith and I even went to church drunk and stoned. By this time I'd been baptised three times. I was searching for God in other religions, but I came to a place in my life where I bowed my knee at the altar when no one was around and cried out to God.

I asked God if he was there to please give me a sign. Weeping and crying like a baby, I got up and went home. The next day I was walking through Cabramatta and a man from the Potter's House [Christian Fellowship] was there handing out their tracts. The flyer read, 'If you're looking for a sign from God, here it is'! It was there in black and white! That was 8 February 2004.

That is miraculous! One day you ask for a sign and the next day you get it.

It was my first supernatural experience. I was with my mates and they said, 'Don't listen to this crap!' I just said, 'You don't know what's going on—you go, I need to deal with something.'

This guy shared with me how Christ loves me and I needed to deal with my sin. For the first time everything started ringing true to me. It was like arrows going straight into my heart and I felt the conviction of God. I knew that even though I believed in God I wasn't going to go to heaven if I died right then. I'd done some bad things. This guy just said, 'Pray with me', right in the middle of the street. So I prayed a prayer that changed the rest of my life.

Was it hard to leave the drugs behind?
It was, and I'm not going to downplay that. But with the backing of heaven you can do anything. It didn't happen overnight for me. I needed to make some hard choices, which meant cutting off some bad influences and not going to some places.

Here I am eight years later—I don't drink, I don't smoke, I don't swear and I'm no longer bound to drugs, gangs or addiction.

And you have four beautiful children.
Yes, all under five years old!

So you find faith in Christ and you say this: 'Christ loved me and his death dealt with my sin and I understood it for the first time.' Why was it so different then, as opposed to your earlier devotional days as a kid in church?
The difference was I never identified with Christ as a man. I now realised God became man and he suffered on the cross as a man, which I can identify with. Then in his resurrection he came alive as God and created in me and in my spirit a hope that I can have a new life. When I prayed a prayer of repentance, confessing with my mouth and believing in my heart, that's when his love flooded me. I had that revelation of who Christ was as a man and God as our Father—that's what changed my life. I would dare to say that I've been through hell and now I'm waiting for heaven!

And now you're passing on all these enormous lessons of life and faith in schools as a chaplain.
Yes. My passion is to bring people to Christ and to make an impact in this generation for the gospel. My heart is for the youth because I understand the issues they go through. Whatever I can do I will

do it. If I can help one soul to a better life, then my job is done—I can go to heaven!

What would you say to the man from the Potter's House if you could speak to him now about what has happened to you?
I actually speak to him regularly. He's an inspiration to my life. If only I could be half the man he is in Christ. I just want to let him know that he's been that great example and I thank him for reaching out to me when no one else did.

Tony, how do you reflect on how different your family's life is now compared with your family's life when you were growing up?
Wow, what a contrast! I now come home from work and I look at my family and I'm the main event! I have four kids tackling me, just having fun. We also talk about all the things that happened in the day. They're just the conversations I guess families should have.

In my family growing up there was none of that. It was all about money—survival. But now it's 'let's enjoy!' I've only got a certain amount of years with my children and I want to be able to prepare them for what is out there. I guess that's a lesson I've learnt growing up: show them when they're young. It's monkey see, monkey gonna do!

It's life more abundant, Leigh, that's what it is, and that's what God has to offer. I never knew that. I always thought it was about religion. The day I was born again, man—God gave me a new life and a life to the full!

Tony Hoang's website is <www.tonyhoang.info>.

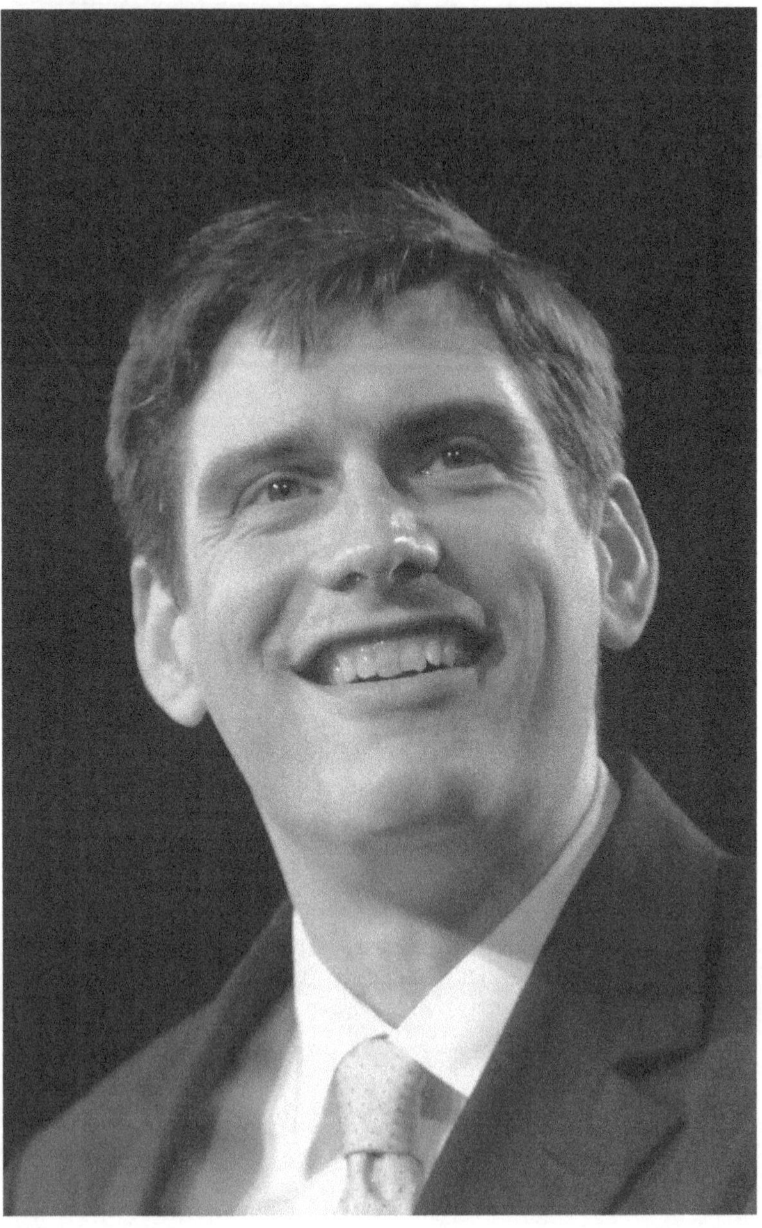

Will Graham

Evangelist and grandson of Billy Graham

At the tender age of five, Will Graham started to realise his grandfather was a bit 'different' from everybody else's. He wondered how it was that so many other people knew his granddaddy.

His grandfather was evangelist Billy Graham, one of the most significant figures in Western Christianity over the last century.

When Will joined us on *Open House*, our conversation explored what it was like living in such a family and following in such large footsteps. He's now likewise touring the world—preaching, evangelising and being a voice for the poor—having previously been happily working away as a local pastor.

I was cutting grass one day in 2006. God just spoke to my heart and said, 'Will, it's time for you to leave the local church.' I didn't want to go—I loved being there. We were in the middle of a building campaign (we were a church plant). They paid me well, they gave me time off, they loved me. But then God called and told me it was time to come and help my father [Franklin Graham].

Working for family is sometimes tough. I love my father, but sometimes it's nice when you can tell your dad 'no'. But I know, even though we've had tough times hitting heads like a father and son do—we're so much alike—I realise that it's God who has called me to do this and so we keep pushing on together.

I think it is notable that the emphasis in and around the Billy Graham organisation has somewhat evolved from the heyday of your grandfather's crusades. With your father's commitment to Samaritan's Purse, the poor of the world are very much on his radar.
It's been on my grandfather's radar all these years, but it's a lot more evident in my father's life, mainly through the work of Samaritan's Purse. My father has always said that God put him in the ditches of life to help the hurting. My dad believes that any time God reveals a need, then God expects you to do something about it—whether it's feeding them, getting them housing, giving them clothes or telling them about Jesus. Whatever it is, you've got to do it. So Samaritan's Purse has worked all around the world, here in Australia as well. It has been a wonderful ministry.

Before we get to talk about your grandfather, can we talk about your dad, Franklin, another world renowned evangelist. He arrived there after running off the rails a bit, didn't he?
Somewhat like Jonah, he ran in the opposite direction. He didn't want to be a preacher—the religion thing wasn't him. He wasn't going to pretend; he just went in the other direction. He loved his mum and dad and respected them, but everybody was trying to make him into a preacher: 'Well, you're Billy Graham's son—you've got to be a preacher!' He just said, 'I don't want to be a preacher.'

So he ran his own life and he went downhill. Anytime you're apart from Christ your life goes downhill.

How did that play out practically in his life?
My dad was actually a pretty good person, but for him it was at least cigarettes and alcohol that were consuming him. Then one day he said, 'I just got sick and tired of being sick and tired.' He knew he had to come back to the Lord. He turned his life over to Jesus Christ. That was in his early twenties, and then he soon got married and then I came along.

Will, can I take you back to the age of five when you started to realise, 'My family seems to be a bit different from all the others'?
I was in the first year of school and one of my teachers came up and said to another teacher, 'Hey, this is Billy Graham's grandson.' I thought, 'Man, how does she know who my granddaddy is?' I didn't know anything.

I went to public school just like every normal kid. All my friends treated me the same—they didn't know who Billy Graham was. They didn't really care. All they wanted to know about was if you had the latest Nintendo game or if you were a good soccer player or football player.

I probably didn't understand the full impact until I got to college. I went to Liberty University, a Christian university. It became pretty evident then. I had a lot of people knocking on my doors wanting to talk about Billy Graham or meet Billy Graham's grandson. I also started to see the impact he had had on the Christian world, so it really changed my outlook about my granddaddy.

What were your strongest early memories of him?
Just being a granddad! He always treats his grandchildren like grandchildren. He never preached at them. He wanted to know

what was going on in your life. Most of my memories were around his crusades. He spent almost his whole life on the road.

Was it a weird thing or more an impressive thing to see your granddaddy up there in front of thousands of people?
I hate to say it, but for me that was normal. It was the only thing I knew. I thought everybody's granddad did this. I had never known a time when I wasn't Billy Graham's grandson.

He's written a book over the past couple of years called Nearing Home, *which is such a poignant title now that he's in his mid-nineties. One thing that struck me in that book was his declaration that growing old is not for the faint-hearted.*
He hates every moment of it. It's the things he wants to do that he can't do any more. It's very hard for him to eat now; his motor skills have declined. The things that you wish you could do yourself, you have to get someone else to help you.

Most of my granddaddy's friends and most of his family members are in heaven. He only has a few close friends left, including Cliff Barrows and George Beverly Shea. They are still a team, but he's longing for heaven.

He must, then, look with such hope to the future if he hates everything of what he is going through at the moment.
It's been tough. But he realises that God has him here for a reason. He still wants to fulfil what God wants him to do, whether it's meeting with people, shaking hands, praying with people, giving people advice or writing books.

Will, your own journey with the Christian faith started very young, with your dad playing an important role.

It did. I remember one particular day I was at church and it happened to be communion Sunday. I was about six or seven years old and not in children's church anymore. Being communion Sunday I was, like, 'Hey, it's grown-ups' snacks! I get what the grown-ups get—some bread and juice—this is great!' I remember my dad saying, 'No, you can't have any.' I guessed it was because he thought I was going to spill the grape juice on the carpet.

When I got home Dad took me up to my room and explained to me why I couldn't have it. It was because I had never asked Jesus to come into my life and forgive me of my sins. And so my father explained that to me. That afternoon I asked Jesus to come into my life.

It wasn't like I was a murderer, but I still knew even at a young age that I needed Jesus in my life if I wanted to spend eternity with God. So I turned my life to Christ that day. It doesn't mean I understood everything about the Bible or theology, but that was when I started putting my faith in Jesus Christ.

I'm so grateful that it happened to me at a young age.

Do you ever have doubts about this faith? Does being in such a family and committed to such an enterprise as the Billy Graham organisation ever allow you to have doubts about that faith?

I'm not sure if doubt is the right word, but there are definitely times that I mess up. I think my biggest doubts arise when I ask, 'God, is this what you want me to be doing? Or is it something else? Do you want me in the local church or working at Samaritan's Purse or working for the Billy Graham Evangelistic Association?' That's probably where I have more doubts: 'Lord, exactly what do you want me to be doing? How do you want me to best serve you?'

Is it much of a juggle for your own personal faith—keeping it real, living and personal—and not being somewhat overwhelmed by the enterprise? Does it ever seem more the faith of an enterprise than something personal?
The Billy Graham Evangelistic Association is a ministry, but that is not a substitute for my own spiritual walk with Jesus Christ. There is no substitute for that. I try to tell people that reading a good book or a good commentary is not a substitute for reading God's word. So I try to spend time in God's word to the best of my ability each and every day.

I'm sure you have reflected on this question: what was it about your grandfather's life that was so significant to the Christian lives of many communities and even nations—for instance, the famous 1959 Crusade in Australia? What was it about that time and what was it about him that God chose to use?
Well, I don't think it was anything about Billy Graham.

I'm sure he would say that too.
This is all about Jesus Christ reaching the people of this world. It was never about Billy Graham. Granted, God used my grandfather, but to be honest it could have been anybody. He just happened to be the person God chose. I think what I love about my grandfather is that he was willing.

When he was a young kid, my grandfather was never dreaming of this stuff. Matter of fact, people often say, 'Why did you travel so hard when you were so young? Why did you do all those crusades, back to back to back in all those places?' He said, 'Because I thought in a few years it was going to be over.' He had no idea it was going to continue.

He never asked for fame, he never asked for money and he never asked for position. He was a dairy farmer—a nobody. There was no Billy Graham before 1949 in the public's eye. No one had heard of him and no one really cared. It was something that he never saw. One of the greatest characteristics of my grandfather is his humility.

But it's not just his humility. The Bible says God gives grace to the humble. Because my grandfather stayed humble before God, God put an extra measure of grace around him like a bubble and Satan couldn't get to him. God said, 'I'm going to bless you, Billy. I'm going to protect you so that you can be my tool to reach a generation all around the world.'

And yet he was sought out by Presidents and many great people.
There have been forty-four US Presidents. My grandfather has known twelve of them—that's over twenty-five per cent.

Of all the things that I'm sure you have learnt from your grandfather, what would you consider to be the top thing?
Any son or grandson wants to please his father and grandfather. I hope that I have always been pleasing to them. But at the end of the day I'm not here to please them; I'm here to please my God, Jesus Christ. So I hope I can honour my grandfather by being faithful to Jesus Christ.

My grandfather has been very faithful to God. He's not been perfect—he's a sinner like any one of us. He has his shortcomings (though they are a lot fewer than most of us!). He's not perfect, and he needs Jesus just like everybody else.

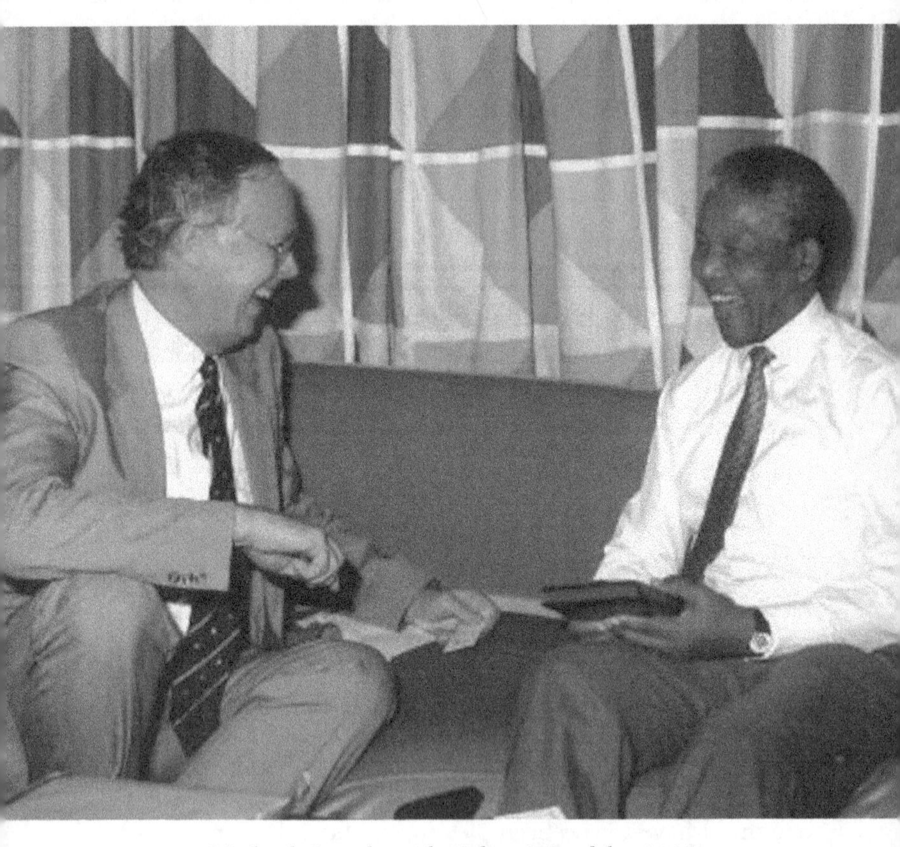

Michael Cassidy with Nelson Mandela, 1992

Michael Cassidy

Founder of African Enterprise

For decades, Michael Cassidy has been a giant of the modern Christian world.

He was born in South Africa and founded the enormously important organisation African Enterprise. Its six hundred staff and countless volunteers and friends operate in seven countries, promoting Christian faith through word and deed.

Michael played a highly significant role in the ending of apartheid in South Africa, and in particular in the country's peaceful transition averting widespread bloodshed.

We began our conversation by going back to one defining moment more than five decades ago on an African beach.

That *was* a moment much to be remembered. It happened as part of a tour which I did around Africa in 1961 with a friend.

I was a student in the States at the time, at Fuller Seminary, and I had begun to feel the calling of God upon my life. I had a great sense that I needed to go over to Africa and 'look it over'—see what the needs, the challenges and the problems were. I put a map of Africa up in my room. I took one city a day for thirty-one days so that every day I prayed for a different city around the continent. Then I began praying systematically for each African country, and asked that one day I would have the opportunity of ministering in those countries.

We travelled the length and breadth of Africa, 50,000 kilometres around the continent that summer. One of the stops was in Monrovia, Liberia, on the west coast of Africa, a very beautiful but troubled country. I went down to the beach and it was pristine, virginal and beautiful. I remember coming up with a really big prayer in my heart: 'God, I'm going to walk fifty steps along this beach and make fifty imprints in the sand, and I want you to give me one year of ministry on the African continent for every footprint I make.' I proceeded then to walk fifty steps along this virginal, beautiful, magical sand, and when I'd made my fifty steps, I paused and looked back and said, 'Lord, I want one year of ministry in Africa for every one of those steps.'

By God's wonderful grace that has exactly happened and been fulfilled.

It might sound an audacious deal with God to say that.

I think God loves us to pray audaciously. I would always rather pray a prayer too big and have him cut it back than pray too small and have the Lord tell me one day, 'Your vision wasn't big enough.'

And you've had your fifty years!

Today I say to the Lord, '*At least* fifty years! Forget about what I prayed on the sand. I want more!' Right now I've asked the Lord to give me another twenty years of ministry.

When you look back now more than five decades on, what has it all taught you about how God works?
I have learnt he takes very weak people. I'm not saying that out of some kind of false modesty. When I left university and before I went to seminary, I would have been too nervous to speak even to a Sunday school class. I had all kinds of social fears, inadequacies, insecurities. Just like when the Lord called Moses, I said to him, 'I can't speak. I'm not up to this.' I couldn't cope with social situations such as parties. I couldn't arrive at the door of a church on a Sunday after the morning church service and say thank you to the minister for the message without my throat constricting, my hands perspiring. I only share this to say that I was completely inadequately prepared or equipped for something like this.

That's why I thought my life would be spent teaching ten and eleven-year-old boys in a little preparatory school. That's how I saw my life. Then it was like the Lord said, 'No, I've got more for you, and if I call you to it, I will equip you.'

In 1957 in the basement of Madison Square Garden during Billy Graham's New York Crusade, I heard the voice of the Lord as distinctively as I ever heard it on anything, and he said, 'I want you to do city evangelism in Africa.' I said to him, 'Listen, Lord, I know you don't mess up too often, but you've messed up now because I'm not up to this!'

Was it a fearful prospect?
Yes, very fearful to me. Then the Lord began to give me confidence. So when you ask what I have learnt—I've learnt that God takes the feeble, the inadequate, the very ordinary and he leads us forward.

He's a God who guides. Psalm 32:8 says, 'I will instruct you and teach you in the way you should go; I'll guide you with my eye upon you.' I've learnt that to be true. I've learnt that God is faithful and standing beside one. I've learnt that he enables us to do what he calls us to do.

Your work is 'to engage the word and deed', combining both dynamics, which is quite a distinctive ministry.
Our mission statement says that we exist 'to evangelise the cities of Africa through word and deed, in partnership with the church'. It's very holistic. You can't go to a person who is starving, for example, and just hand them a tract about John 3:16. You can't go in after genocide in Rwanda and just preach from an air-conditioned pulpit. You are speaking to broken and smashed up people, aching at the most profound levels of their beings. Our Lord combined both of these aspects in his work. We see it like the two wings of a bird or the two blades of a pair of scissors—they belong together.

Michael, I'd love you to take us through the critical part that you and African Enterprise played in the lead-up to the 1994 elections in South Africa that ended apartheid. This was a nation on the brink.
Things were going from bad to worse in the country. Every aeroplane was filled with what we called PFP's, 'People Packing for Perth'. There was the most enormous exodus, the most tremendous fear. The country was drifting towards a kind of civil war. Nothing the politicians were doing seemed able to resolve it.

As we were moving along through those years something became evident to me: that many of our leaders had similar visions for the future of South Africa, but they were all in different hermetically sealed political parties and never spoke to each other. A group of us from African Enterprise visited all the different political parties and prayed with them. We found that here were people with a similar language, similar vision, but they were not talking together.

After we had prayed with them we said we needed to try and get some of these people together. We mounted dialogue weekends at a place called Kolobe Game Lodge. We had about fifteen to twenty different political leaders at each of these weekends. There was a handful of Christians as well as Muslims, communists, secularists and atheists. I think many of them came very suspicious, wondering what Michael was up to. But I said, 'No, all we want you to do is to share your own story, and then, secondly, your vision of a new South Africa, and then, thirdly, the steps to reach it.

For many of them it was almost an intoxicating experience. They'd never spoken to others about their political stories. There is something very powerful about hearing someone's story. Once I hear your story, you are demythologised to me. The stereotypes I may put round you break because I now hear what actually makes you tick. So huge transformation took place in the lives of many of these political leaders. They came as enemies and left as friends.

So here we are coming into the end of 1993 and we've got this network of friends in place, but the country is still going from bad to worse. We're heading towards the April 27 elections and the country is burning. In my area twenty people a day were dying—up to ninety every weekend. At this point then President de Klerk, Dr Mandela and Prince Mangosuthu Buthelezi decided they needed to call in international mediators led by Henry Kissinger and the British Foreign Secretary, Lord Carrington. After only twenty-four hours the process broke down. Kissinger said Armageddon would be there in two weeks' time. The US State Department had told us they were anticipating one million dead.

We called a prayer meeting the next day in Kings Park rugby stadium. We didn't know whether five would come or fifty or five hundred. In the event twenty-five thousand people turned out to pray. As South Africa cried representatively in that prayer meeting to God to bring an answer, in the VIP lounge we had Jacob Zuma (now President of South Africa), representing Mandela; we had Prince Mangosuthu Buthelezi himself; and we had Mr Danie Shutte, the man in charge of the South African elections, representing President de Klerk. That evening by about a quarter to nine these men had reached an agreement on a document, finalised within the bowels of this prayer meeting.

That was April 17. On April 18 they dotted i's and crossed t's, and on April 19 de Klerk, Buthelezi and Mandela came on the media and said, 'We've found a way through for South Africa.' None of us will ever, ever forget the emotion of that. The media had no language to describe it other than the language of faith. So every editorial was headed 'Miracle', 'Miracle', 'Miracle', 'Miracle'. The *Natal Daily News* headline was 'The day God stepped in to save South Africa'. The *Wall Street Journal* carried a full page on God and politics. TIME Magazine said, 'If there are miracles in history, this is one.' The BBC said, 'We are witness to an authentic miracle in history.' The elections were less than a week away, and the elections happened in the three most peaceful days probably in the history of South Africa after all of that violence.

So we know that God stepped in—the Lord had pulled it off.

Can you share with us what Nelson Mandela was like to deal with and to relate to through that time?

Mandela is a most extraordinary man. One was struck by the graciousness of the man, the humility of the man. He told us how when he was in prison he never failed to go to the Bible study or to the church service or the communion. Those twenty-seven years on Robben Island should have set him up to come out with all guns blazing for bitterness, for revenge, for slaughtering every white. But I think Mandela saw that an eye for an eye makes everybody blind. Forgiveness would be the answer. Of course, he then established the Truth and Reconciliation Commission where amnesty was given in exchange for truth.

He is a very remarkable person. A lot of grace, a lot of charisma. The spirit of reconciliation was on him. And certainly, when he became president, I felt he was *my* president. Somehow or other he embraced the whites. They were halcyon days politically, and the New South Africa was being born.

Throughout your very significant ministry, you have had a deep and ongoing connection with two giants: Billy Graham and John Stott. Are there two things, one from each, that you learnt or that particularly impacted on your life?
It's true I have always said that those were the two men who most significantly shaped my own life and ministry. I've had the privilege of knowing them and loving them dearly. Billy Graham is still alive and I pray for him daily. I prayed daily for John Stott while he was alive and now thank God for him every day.

I think with Billy Graham the thing I would probably want to identify with is his faithfulness to the gospel. Billy Graham is an absolutely faithful proclaimer of the biblical message, no matter what is happening around him. He believed that people without Christ were lost and he preached with a tremendous urgency and passion.

The other thing I would pick out about Billy Graham is his integrity. When all those televangelists were collapsing with all those dramas in the States some years ago, TIME Magazine, which is not a Sunday school journal, came up in its religion section with an article entitled 'And then there was Billy'. I wrote to Billy Graham after that and said, 'Billy, I just thank God for your integrity. You've ploughed a straight furrow morally, financially, practically, and in every way you have been true blue. You've been the real thing. Thank you for that.'

With John Stott, one of the things that always struck me about him was diligence of presentation and depth of content. John Stott would spend one hour for every five minutes of public speaking in preparation. Most of us throw a talk together in a few minutes. Not John—he would have a diligence of preparation. And the consequence of that was he would have a true depth of biblical content. To me, Stott on content and Billy on spirit—I would love, in the best of all possible worlds, to bring those things together in my own life's ministry.

openhouse
openhouse
openhouse

Benny Perez

Founder of the Church of South Las Vegas

My guess is most of us could hardly contemplate facing up to the potentially life-shattering challenges that Pastor Benny Perez and his wife Wendy have faced over the past few years. The interesting thing is that those challenges came in the wake of wave after wave of success in their lives.

More than that, those successes were happening in the name of God. Pastor Benny felt called by God to set up a new church, the Church of South Las Vegas, USA. It began with twenty-seven people but today numbers more than three thousand.

Pastor Benny is quick to say that he's not about numbers, but his was a ministry truly blessed by God for the great benefit of lots of people in Las Vegas. Then Easter 2010 changed everything.

We started our church right there in our house, growing from twenty-seven to three thousand-plus people. I think it's been the grace of God and the timing of God. I point to the Scripture that says, 'God uses the base things, the things that people would not normally choose, to confound the wise.' It's been a really awesome move of God that's taken place.

Can I ask you how you viewed the people of Las Vegas and how might that have differed from other churches in the city—that there were so many people who flocked to your church?
I like Las Vegas because the people there are not religious. In America they have the 'Bible belt' where everybody goes to church and everybody thinks they know God. Well, Vegas is known as 'Sin City'! People say, 'I'm not religious at all, but if you're telling me that this Jesus loves me and wants me and can do something in my life—man, that's the kind of Jesus I want!'

So we didn't preach a judgmental Jesus. We preached the Jesus of the Bible, the friend of sinners. And they started coming. The only ones that get upset are the Pharisees!

Do you mean other church people?
I think our biggest challenge, even in our church, hasn't been the people who have gotten saved. It's the people who have been saved but now forget the grace of God that touched them. They say things like, 'How can God reach people like strippers?' I simply tell people that Jesus saves them. The gospel is good news, which means 'come as you are'; but the power of the gospel means you won't stay as you are. And there is a process in that. So we allow people to move through that process, and the Holy Spirit is the one that brings change. Jesus is making a difference.

It's actually a process for all of us, over our entire lives.
Absolutely! I think some people want to speed up the process for others because they see this innate sin in other people. We have to be careful and remember that God is always working in all of us, for the rest of our lives.

So Las Vegas, 'Sin City', wealth, glamour, entertainment, glitz—what's it really like?
There are over two million people who live there. It's like any other city, raising families, doing life. It's a dichotomy: you have this little place called 'The Strip' and you have two million people living around it. It's almost like two worlds in one city.

There is a price to pay for lots of people with all that glitz and glamour.
Yes. The motto is 'What happens in Vegas stays in Vegas', but that's not true. What happens in Vegas goes home with you. So there are a lot of stories of people being broken and getting sucked into the system. Yet God's grace is there to pull them out.

So here you are powering along, working for God, and it certainly appears you've been richly blessed by him. Then Easter 2010 comes along and initially it was a very happy time for you and your wife.
Yes, it was. My wife was four months pregnant and we were getting ready to have nine worship services to reach nine thousand people. We went for a simple ultrasound for my wife's pregnancy. Little did we know we'd be seeing such devastation that it would consume the next two years of our lives.

We'd previously had a miscarriage and my wife was a little bit concerned. She was doing great after four months. And there on the screen, the heart beat was great. We saw the baby in the womb—170 beats a minute and everything was great. Then the heart beat dropped down to 150, then 130 and then 100. The technician went out to get the doctor, who came in and said, 'It seems like there might be some challenges here.' The heart beat then went down to 70. I'm saying, 'Something is not right here', and literally before our eyes—it was devastating—it went from 50 to 30 to 20 and then it flat-lined.

In thirty years the doctor said they had never seen a baby flat-line on the screen. Now people say, 'Oh well, it was just a miscarriage—you never held the baby.' But we held the baby in our hearts and it was devastating.

It was the Wednesday before Good Friday, and I had to preach nine times. My wife was devastated. I was in denial. We just packed up and went back to the house.

I didn't sleep that night and just prayed. We went back the next morning because I wanted another ultrasound. I was thinking, 'We're approaching Resurrection Sunday and maybe God is going to do a miracle.' They did it first thing in the morning and there was no blood flow. It verified that the baby was dead.

They scheduled emergency surgery for Good Friday morning. My wife had complications on the table. She was released and I got her home and that's when we literally almost lost her. When we got home, she collapsed in my garage, bleeding out. I called the emergency number and the operator said, 'Keep her awake! You can't let her go unconsciousness.' So here I am praying, waiting for the ambulance to come, and it was the longest three minutes of my life. They rushed her back to the hospital, and by the grace of God there was the right person in emergency who was able to do a procedure on her that stabilised her and saved her life.

Then she said to me, 'You know what, Benny? You need to go and preach. Don't let this stop us. Don't let this stop what God wants you to do.' So I got home at four o'clock in the afternoon, showered, went to the church and sat at my desk at six o'clock. I said, 'Lord, I know it's always been you, but it's got to be you now.'

I actually preached ten times that weekend. That Good Friday I preached the message differently, because on Good Friday the Father lost his Son and on that Good Friday I lost my daughter. I felt the heart of a father losing a child, and I realised the great price that Jesus paid and the Father paid for you and for me. I think I preached the gospel message more clearly and from the heart of a father than I ever had in my life.

As a result of that, over ten worship services we had more than one thousand people respond to trust Jesus with their life. It was Resurrection Weekend in Las Vegas!

Nobody knew what had happened to us. The church didn't know; none of my staff knew. Only two of my executive pastors knew because we didn't want to distract from the weekend. Everybody found out the following Monday and Tuesday. They were saying things like, 'Pastor, I don't even know how you preached.' I just said it was the grace of God.

As time goes on, you understandably keep crying out to God, 'Why?' Have you had any idea of what the answer to that might be?
No. In all my theological training, my Bible colleges and my studies, you're never supposed to ask why. I understand the sovereignty of God, but in my humanness, in my humanity . . . I think everybody deep down in the depths of their hearts at times cries out, 'Why?'

But at the end of the day, Leigh, it wasn't so much about the why. God said, 'You know, son, it's not about the why, it's about the who.' That 'who' was Jesus. Sometimes God's not going to answer your question, but he gives you something better. He gives you a person.

The Bible says that God draws near to those with a broken heart and a crushed spirit [Psalm 34:18]. The book of 2 Corinthians says,

'With the comfort that God has comforted you, comfort others.' That comfort comes from a person, the person of Jesus.

So an unexpected answer but still a satisfying and comforting one?
Absolutely. Absolutely. Why did we lose that baby? Why did we suffer all these things? That was just the first of a multiplicity of challenges and storms. Every time, just like the disciples in the boat in the middle of the storm, [it would have been easy to ask], 'Why is this storm happening?' We didn't know why the storm happened, but the 'who' showed up and his name was Jesus.

It's important to say this, that Jesus being 'the way, the truth and the life' is not just a platitude or a cute religious answer.
Christianity is about a relationship. It's a Person, not principles. I don't fall in love with theology—I've fallen in love with, and I receive the love of, a Person. This wasn't me loving God. The Bible says you don't love God first but that he loves you and sent his only Son as a total sacrifice for your sin.

You've written powerfully about this whole experience and the lessons you and your wife learnt in your book More: Discovering the God of more when life gives you less. *That's a curious title!*
It's an oxymoron, isn't it—that more comes out of less? But God is more. God is the strength of our life when we are weak. Paul puts it this way: when you are weak, when you are less, God is more. 'When I am weak, then I am strong' [2 Corinthians 12:10]. He was giving us more strength, more comfort, more grace, and in that I realised that God is the one who was bringing us through. My faith was not empowered by me—it was powered by him.

It can take people some time to get that view, or to know the reality of that. You might have to wait and trust.

Absolutely. This is not a quick fix. I just prayed, 'Trust in the Lord with all your heart and lean not on your own understanding. In all your ways acknowledge him and he will make your paths straight' [Proverbs 3:5–6]. If you want to be God's person, you have to go through God's process many times.

Tommy Emmanuel

Guitar supremo

Guitar legend Tommy Emmanuel has been entertaining and delighting audiences around the world for more than five decades. He began being paid as a performer when he was six—two bottles of Coke a gig!

We had a delightful, revealing and wide-ranging conversation about a life lived for many years in grinding poverty and all the way through to world-wide fame. Tommy is an Aussie treasure, with a special passion to pass on all his lessons of life to the next generation of young musicians and performers. If ever there was a person who has travelled the 'long and winding road', it's Tommy Emmanuel.

I can remember being around people in the [Sydney] Showground, watching entertainers really do something to the audience. I also remember the first person who had a powerful impact on me from the stage and that was [veteran Australian rocker] Col Joye. That was a long, long time ago—1960. I was five years old. That's the first time I witnessed somebody with that much charisma.

Tommy, paint us a picture of your family troupe, because it was very much a family affair on the road.
It was Mum and Dad and six children. I was the youngest on stage. We had my older brother Chris hitting drums, my sister Virginia played Hawaiian steel guitar and my brother Phil, of course, as the main lead player. I was the accompanist and the showman out the front. I was the one who would communicate with the audience a lot, the one who moved around. The others were pretty much static.

We didn't know any other way of life. What you have to remember is that we were little kids and we could actually play music on our instruments. We weren't taught by some Suzuki method or something else. We were self-taught players who were finding our own way. What we were doing was well beyond our years. I think that brought an element of surprise for the audience. That gift is something precious to me and something I honour every night and stay dedicated to.

Tommy, can you paint us a picture of your mum and dad?
Well, I don't remember much about Dad because he died when I was very young, but I do remember him bragging nauseatingly about us. We were so broke all the time. We were always enlisting help from here and there. People were really wonderful to us.

My mother was an angel who walked the earth. She provided for us in such an amazing way. We were incredibly poor, but we kids didn't know it. My mother could cook a shoe and make it taste good! In fact, we ate shoe quite often! When we ran out of money and we were totally destitute, my mother would get out the rice and boil it up and put a bit of powdered milk on it and a bit sugar. That's what we lived on until we earned some money. We basically lived from week to week on the road. There were times when we did pretty well and we enjoyed that.

In the old days, in the early '60s, we just had a tent and a station wagon. All the rivers in Australia were full of fish and they were clean, so we camped by the river, did our washing there and bathed ourselves in the river. We'd drink the water and we'd eat the fish—it was ideal really.

Your mum thought that music was good for your health.
She did. She said that playing music would keep you well, keep you young, keep you inspired and it was good for you in life in general. She was right in so many ways. Playing music for people and entertaining them, young and old, is a wonderful thing. I still feel that way. It's a great privilege because you play music for people and they get happy. That is a wonderful thing.

Tommy, somewhere in the midst of this you went to Sunday school as a kid, which meant a great deal to you.
It was mostly with my grandmother. She was a wonderful, wonderful old lady. My grandmother and my grandfather were just very quiet living, humble people.

Did that stick with you for long through those years on the road and then ultimately when you started to get some success in the Big Smoke?
I think I've always been a family-oriented person. I come from a very simple up-bringing. The codes that I live by have never changed.

I read a quote of yours that had a sense of 'I'm not running this ship'. Your job was to get up and play the guitar and let God do the rest.
That's right. It's an illusion in this world that we are in control.

We are in control of absolutely nothing. Our job is to take what gifts we have been given, show up and do our best with them for the benefit of others. That's what our real job is—to help each other. That's why we're here.

If ever you've had a sense of not being in control, it was the loss of your dad at the age of eleven. Then comes the memorable and important connection in your life with the American guitarist and performer Chet Atkins. How did that come about?
I wrote him a fan letter and he wrote back to me, and we just stayed in touch. It was unbelievable that this idol, this greatest player on the planet, took the time to write to some kid from nowhere. That inspired me so much. We became friends. We ended up recording together and working together. That was a fulfilment of my dream.

It's a wonderful story. There was one particular song that captured your imagination called 'Windy and Warm'. What was it about that particular song that struck you?
In that song I could hear that Chet was playing everything at once. People said, 'Oh no, it's a recording trick, it's them damn Yankees!' Nobody believed it was just one guy. But I did. I thought, 'Whatever he's doing there, that's what I've got to do.'

The funny thing is that years later, when I got to know Chet very well, he told me he'd had the exact same experience. He was living on a farm down in Columbus, Georgia, with his father and stepmother. He heard Merle Travis on the radio and said to himself, 'Whatever that is, that's what I've got to do.'

So you set about learning that purely by ear and nailed it?
I had to work it out. There was nobody who could play that way in

this country in those days. I struggled to work out what was going on, but I eventually got hold of it. It was like someone lit a fire under me and I found something that I could really work towards. I eventually worked out how to play the tunes—the bass part, the rhythm part and the melody part all at the same time. I would do it on stage, and people would be so amazed they'd be looking for the tape recorder behind the curtain!

So you are back out on the road after the death of your dad with your mum and you six kids. Then child welfare tracks you down and that's it for the road.
Yes, they forced us off the road. They didn't really believe that we were getting a good education, which was a shame because we were getting a very good education. Our mother was seeing to that.

Anyway, things unfold—you can only join the dots of your life when you look back. So with us going to school, Phil my brother and I formed another band, and then we got on television and all that kind of stuff. We ended up working together in other bands as well. I was in my early teens and I was starting to gain a clarity that if I worked harder on my instrument, if I practised a lot, I could really do the things that I thought were impossible. A light came on for me and I got really dedicated and really got it to work.

So as soon as you can get out of Parkes, where your family has been living, you head to the Big Smoke of Sydney, and you start to land some pretty enviable gigs and music sessions. Drop some names for us—who were you working with then?
In the early days I was musical director for a guy named Lionel Long. Then I became musical director for John Farnham and then I worked with everybody from Marcia Hines, Renee Geyer,

Doug Parkinson to John English and Air Supply. I ended up playing on some American records at that time too because there were producers who came out to Australia who had heard about me. So it was a nice thing to play on a Roberta Flack album. I did a track on a Diana Ross album. And then more recently I got to play on the Michael Jackson album that came out after Michael died.

Is there one particular opportunity or performance that stands out head and shoulders above the others?
Recording with Chet Atkins was a great time for me and an absolute dream come true. But I still think my mountain-top experience, apart from playing on Michael Jackson's track, would have to be playing at the closing ceremonies of the Olympic Games with my brother.

Tommy, this may seem such a basic question musically, but my guess is it's a critical one. How much do you practise? I expect your brilliant performance is backed up by solid practise behind the scenes.
Absolutely. I practise as often as I can and as often as I need to. Sometimes there's a real need to work on your skills. For instance—and here is a classic example—today with my sound check, my hands weren't as good as they were earlier today. They had got cold and I think they'd slowed down a little. So before the show tonight, I need to really warm up. I need to go into the bathroom in my dressing room and play real hard for about half an hour and really get the blood into my hands. I work on skills all the time. I work on strength, control, improvising and things like that. I do a lot of different stuff.

Can I ask you to reflect back on that very special relationship you had with Chet Atkins and what he did for you—not just musically but for your character as well?

Chet taught me a lot about how to treat people. It didn't matter if you were the President or the waiter at the restaurant, you got treated the same. He was a real gentleman and a very caring and loving 'daddy' to me. He was also a straight shooter. He said things as they were. He was brutally honest. Just being around him was inspiring—he was a really great man.

I've known other people like that here in Australia. I could say the same thing about Col Joye and Slim Dusty.

It has all given you a particular passion to give something back to the next generation.

Absolutely. There are so many great young players around the planet now—my goodness, they're everywhere! I meet young people every night when I do what we call a 'meet and greet' before every show. An hour before show time I meet the public, instead of coming out after the show. That gives me an opportunity to hear those young ones who bring their guitar and who want to play. I get a chance to hear them and talk with them intimately. That gives me a good energy for the show!

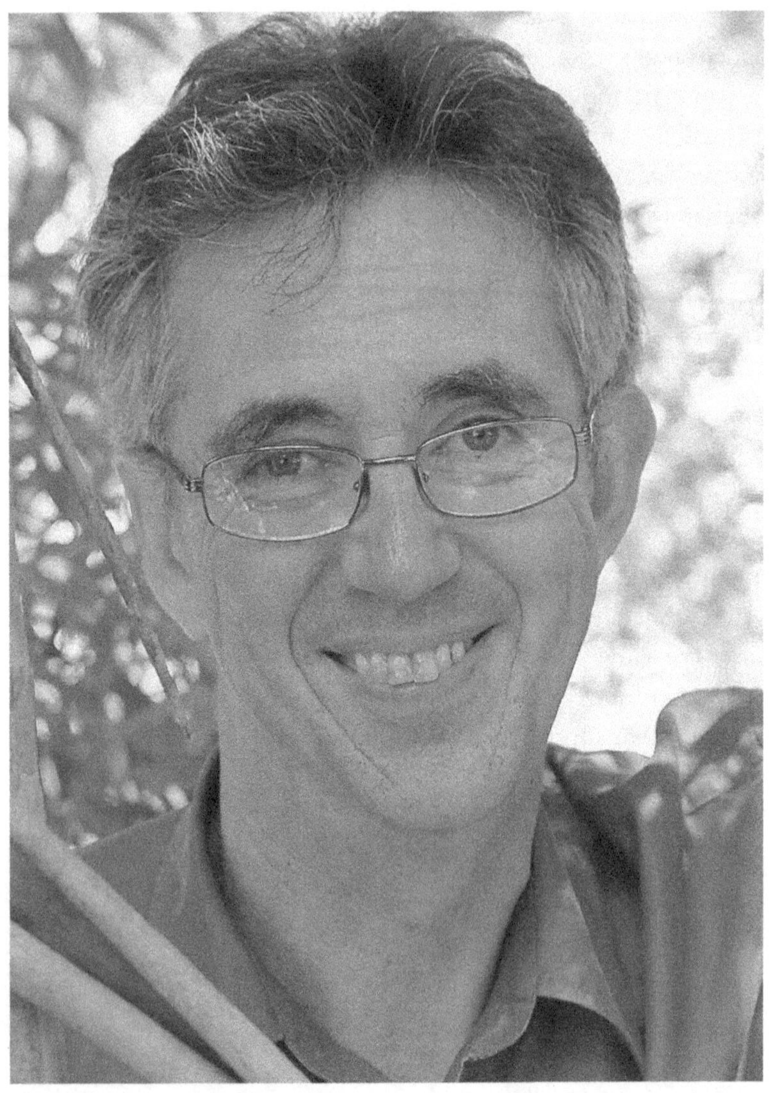

Steve Biddulph

'Raising Girls'

It's been one of the great privileges of my life to help raise three gorgeous girls in our family. It's a huge responsibility. No one does it perfectly. Today especially it's a very tricky task to navigate—particularly if you're a dad!

That's why Steve Biddulph's thoughts on raising girls are a gift to parents and girls around Australia—and around the world.

Steve's ground-breaking book *Raising Boys* sold three million copies worldwide. Now he's addressing the emotional and physical development, education, social conditioning and relationships of girls in *Raising Girls*.

It was a privilege to dip into his vast wisdom when he joined us on *Open House*.

When I first wrote *Raising Boys*, it was no great surprise that boys had been in trouble for hundreds of years. But there was a 'boy catastrophe' unfolding when I first started looking at them. For instance, boys have three times the death rate of girls in the under twenty-five age range.

I had assumed, and this was twenty years ago, that girls were doing just fine. And in fact, girls were educationally and in all kinds of ways soaring ahead, because we put a lot of work into them during the twentieth century.

Then about five or six years ago we started getting research and statistical evidence from around the world, particularly in mental health epidemiology, that was pointing to a sudden drop off in the mental health of girls. It looks like about one in five girls now has some kind of really serious mental health problem—whether it's an eating disorder, binge drinking, a lot of anxiety, depression or body image issues. We are now very, very worried about girls. It's not every girl, but we are now getting activated to help parents fight back.

So why do you think it's been happening in this recent generation?
About ten years ago corporations around the world began to recognise that there was a very lucrative market in selling products to young women, especially if they targeted what they now call the pre-teens. They identified the pre-teens (sometimes called the 'tweens') as girls from about eight up to about twelve or thirteen. One of the things we know about girls is that they are very socially aware, very conscious of belonging and fitting in. These companies realised that if they could get these young girls anxious about their looks, about belonging and being lovable, they could create a huge market for selling things like fashion products, diet products, makeup and things like that.

When you and I were kids, Leigh, if a girl was going down to the shops on a Saturday morning, she would probably put on some clean jeans and a T-shirt, she'd brush her hair and she'd be off. These days, girls of twelve or thirteen spend an hour putting themselves together with makeup and fretting about what to wear.

And the message is: you're not good enough as you are.
That's exactly the message. 'Your looks are the most important thing about you.' What gets blasted into young girls is that looks are everything. If you don't look perfect or like you're the front of a magazine when you step out the door, you won't be good enough. It's also now crossing over to boys as well.

In the research they're asked, 'What is your biggest concern?' Seventy per cent of young people write 'my looks'.

Isn't the message from parents about their worth and identity strong enough? Surely that could reassure them.
I'm glad you're looking at it in that broad picture, Leigh, because that is the other half of the problem. We've also begun to realise that we just have not loved our girls well enough. First of all, you need to ask how you stop the toxic media coming at your daughter. Second, how do you make her strong enough so that it all just washes off?

Fifty years ago aunties were a really big part of the lives of girls. Sometimes you would be embarrassed about sharing with your mum or you'd be angry with her, but if you didn't want to talk to her, there were nearly always two or three aunties around. Girls and aunties used to be allies in life, and aunties could talk sense to the girls. Over the last fifty years older women have disappeared from our girl's lives. So you've got mum, you've got the odd school teacher that a girl gets on well with, but after that it's just the peer group. Peer groups are a very mixed bag. They have the good friends and the caring friends, but there's also a lot of meanness, competition and quite a lot of pain. It's too much burden to put on a group of sixteen-year-olds to look after the mental health of each other.

So I want to start an 'auntie movement' where anyone who's got nieces starts to take them out for coffee and meet them every month, has them over to their house for weekends and becomes a real active presence in their niece's lives. I think this might be part of the 'immunisation' of our daughters.

I've also got this thing I say to audiences sometimes, that 'hurry is the enemy of love'. We rush past each other more and more at the breakfast table and at dinner time, heading out to meetings and all sorts of things. The love starts to seep out of our family. It is quite common now for people to have a baby but not really spend a lot of time with them. It's in those little things you say when you're bathing your baby—bath time can be just so lovely. That kind of soft, loving time is a lifelong mental health resource.

What I'm telling people is that we know from psychology that your child would rather have you than have the money. If people have been thinking along those lines themselves and then someone like me comes along and says it, sometimes it's enough to turn a corner.

There was a rule we were taught as family therapists called the five per cent rule. Five per cent change is really as much as you can handle. So try to make a five per cent change in how affectionate you are with your children, or spend five per cent more time hanging about before you rush out the door. See whether it makes a difference.

Steve, the birth of your own daughter sparked quite a surprising reaction in you, something that you found very powerful and scary at the same time.

People had said to me, 'What do you want [the baby to be]?' I always said, 'I don't care, I don't mind', and I really believed that.

Our daughter was born by emergency caesarean. When they lifted her out of Sharon's belly and said, 'Oh, it's a girl' I just started bawling—like, 'YES! It's a girl!' All of a sudden the doors in my heart opened and I realised that I really, really wanted a daughter and had never admitted that to myself.

Steve, you say the first year of a girl's life is much more significant than many parents realise. What happens in that crucial first year?
The first year's decision is, 'Am I loved or not? Am I loved and secure?' That little girl looks from her mum's eyes to her dad's eyes. She monitors in her body their heartbeat and their breathing (girl babies are much more alert to the emotions of the people around them) and she decides, 'Is this world a safe place? Are the adults safe? Does Mum love Dad? When people are around me, do they settle down, and can I really, really relax?' So she is making a life conclusion about the world. She doesn't care if she lives in a mansion or in a tin hut. She cares a lot about the emotional quality around them.

Following on from that is the much debated question of how to juggle work and family life and the issue of child care. What's your message to parents about that?
It's not just my message; it's what the research says. There is a very, very clear indication that it helps to delay child care as long as you can. When they measure cortisol, a stress by-product in our blood stream, kiddies in day care have very high levels when they first go there. Six months later their stress level hasn't fallen. It turns out that kiddies learn to cope on the outside but can carry stress that we don't know about. A child at home gets progressively more

relaxed as the day goes on. A child in day care gets progressively more uptight.

I realise lots of parents have to put kiddies in day care. After about the age of three they are much more ready for that, but it's not the ideal.

One of the significant points you emphasise is the role of fathers in the raising of girls. This, of course, is not to take anything away from mums, but you're also very keen for dads to step up to this task of raising girls.

Yes. Christian speakers in particular got onto it early that dads are in the self-esteem departments for daughters. Mum is the security department, but dad's the opposite sex. As they get into their teens, the opposite sex is the one they are interested in, so they take their cue from their dad as to how interesting they are and how intelligent they are.

It's the simple things, like a dad going to Bunnings on a Saturday morning and on the way home stopping for a hot chocolate with his daughter to have a chat. She can't help but conclude from that that he likes her company. We know, again from the research, that that kind of girl is probably going to wait an extra two years before she has her first sexual experience. She wants men who respect her, and she will have a sense of self-respect. So dads have quite an amazing mental health benefit if they are friendly and interested.

What would you say about the need to spiritually develop a girl (or, for that matter, a boy)?

I think the thing to realise is there is an age that is very open to this. From ages ten to fourteen girls are looking for their soul.

Quite often they are very affected by how bad the world is around them—the poverty, the pollution, the loss of nature. So their spirituality needs to find its channel. Jesus wasn't someone who sat around singing hymns or writing books about stuff. He was on about confronting poverty and injustice, so the people who followed him were activists. I think that's what girls like to see. The kind of spirituality they want is: 'What can I do in this world?' Spirituality is about the big picture.

There has been another great debate over the phrase (one that especially applies to girls and young women) that they can 'have it all', particularly in connection with parenting and careering. How do you respond to that?

I don't think anyone can have it all. I think we are living in the most infantile culture that has ever lived. The role models are people who swan about all day and do nothing, like a world of babies. Only a baby would believe that you can have it all.

What an adult thinks is that things come at a cost. What makes you an adult is when you decide to be in this world for each other. That's what we're called to do, to be here for each other. I think girls have a heart feeling of that, and they are disillusioned if the adults around them are not something to look up to.

Details about Steve's book *Raising Girls* can be found at <www.stevebiddulph.com>.

Richard Gill

CONDUCTOR, EDUCATOR, MAESTRO

Richard Gill is one of the most passionate people I've ever met. I've had the privilege of knowing him for about forty-five years. He was the music teacher at my high school, Marsden High, and for one glorious, inspirational year, my piano teacher.

Infinitely more importantly, Richard went on to a range of highly significant roles in the world of music—in particular classical music and opera. He's a regular conductor of Australia's major orchestras. He's held a range of roles with OzOpera and Victorian Opera. He is the founder of the magnificent Baby Proms; wrote a Top 40 song; conducted David Helfgott's first spectacular return concert; and was a regular on the ABC's *Spicks and Specks*. It's been a full and rich life, and countless numbers of people (including me) have in turn enjoyed a rich musical life thanks to Richard Gill.

He's now brought it all together in a magnificent memoir, *Give Me Excess of It*, which for the first time also tells the story of his early school days. It's a disturbing story that I believe we all need to hear.

The title *Give Me Excess of It* came from the opening lines of *Twelfth Night*: 'If music be the food of love, play on/Give me excess of it.' The title also reflects me a little bit because I am a creature of excess. Moderation is not in my vocabulary! That's something for which I've suffered, but that's fine.

You were no child prodigy, though—it wasn't until thirteen that you began formal music lessons. However, as a child you were intoxicated by the music and ceremony of the Roman Catholic Mass.

I went to school just after the end of World War 2 and the Mass was still in Latin. There was still an element of mystery and ritual. Priests dressed up and there were altar boys, incense, bells and smells, and the choir. As far as I was concerned it was a real theatrical production. When I heard that music and singing, it resonated with me in a spectacular way.

You actually built an altar in your back yard at one time.

I did. I think I probably wanted to be the Pope at some stage! I loved the idea of being in charge and being up the front. I relegated the girl next door, Wilma, to behind the altar because in those days women were not allowed on the altar. Wilma played on a piece of corrugated iron with a stick—that was the organ. I would give the sermon and I would frequently preach to the chooks because the altar was built near a chook yard.

And you recited 'Hail Mary, full of grapes'?

Yes. 'Hail Mary, full of grapes', because that's what I thought it was. We all know 'Hail Mary, full of grace, blessed is the fruit of thy womb'. So 'grapes' and 'fruit of thy womb' were very powerful images for a young child.

Tell me about this day: 28 June 1955. Your first piano arrived at home.

It was my youngest brother Chris's birthday. I came home from school and there was a piano that had been delivered during the day, which was amazing. It was an old Steck, a dual piano/pianola, and it was in a terrible condition. To me it was like heaven!

Fast forward into your twenties. What drew you to music education and not performance?
I thought I would be a performer at some stage, until I was told that I would never be a performer! I didn't ever feel that teaching was a bad second.

I did my very first high school teaching prac at Marsden High School in 1962, and I'll never forget that experience. That's when I knew that teaching was really special. The idea of convincing adolescents that music was a worthwhile pursuit for its own sake was completely and utterly irresistible. I was hooked on music education from that moment. The general interest in music from the school and the school community was really strong. We were seen as one of the leading musical schools in the state.

So why do you say children need music? What's so important about it?
I think the thing that is important about music is that it operates in the abstract. It takes kids to a very, very high level of thinking. Children have to focus, concentrate and listen very hard. All this overlaps into all other areas of learning.

It actually activates areas of the brain different from lots of other learning, doesn't it?
I'm no neuroscientist, but I read quite widely on this topic. Neuroscientists are very, very interested in why music operates differently from all the other arts, and particularly when a child is reading. When you are singing or reading music, both

sides of your brain light up. Not only do they light up, they light up in a rapid sequence from side to side all over the brain. We know that has a really powerful effect on all other areas of learning.

You went on from Marsden to the UK and then to America, into the worlds of conducting and your great passion, opera. What did you take away from Marsden?
From Marsden I sowed the seed for the rest of my life. I learned, for example, that telling somebody that something is good does not convince them. They have to find that out for themselves.

There is an enormous wealth of music. The richness of the repertoire is in hip hop and pop, rock and jazz, opera and classical—it's extraordinary. We don't mind the rubbish because it enables us to discern good from bad. So I learnt from Marsden that if you can teach a child to discriminate and be wise about choices, that's an important lesson.

You also took away from Marsden a wife—we have to mention Maureen! There's a touching dedication at the front of your book: 'Without Maureen there would have been no memories.'
That's true. When I was writing the book, it's not that I didn't think about Maureen, but the editor said, 'Look, we know lots about music, we know lots about your dog Louie, but we haven't heard much about your wife!' I know I could not have done anything without her. That's why that dedication is there—she is very special.

Richard, I think it's really important for us to hear of your early school life and its impact on you—an impact that has continued for the rest

of your life. This was a Roman Catholic school in the late '40s through to the '50s, beginning when you were aged five. Describe for us what that was like for you.
I was desperate to go to school. What I wasn't prepared for was the savagery and the violence, even as very young children. There was a type of psychological abuse that I didn't recognise as psychological abuse—I was five, for crying out loud!

For example, in my very first class, taught by a nun, the children were divided into three blocks 'VG', 'G' and 'H'—which stood for very good, good and hopeless. And I was in the back row of the hopeless block. I was one of the youngest kids in the class. I didn't actually know what hopeless meant.

The Catholic Church is having a very bad time at the moment, and I have to say it's about time. It wasn't just the Catholic Church but all institutions that abused kids—and not just sexually, but psychologically and physically as well.

I was caned when I went to Marist Brothers Eastwood, along with lots of kids, every day of my life from the age of seven to the age of fifteen. Some of those canings were for ignorance—if you didn't know something, you were caned.

For instance, a wrong answer to mental arithmetic?
Correct. I had a doctor visit me at home at my mother's request because she thought I had leukaemia. I was grey and God knows what else. I had a blood test and I was absolutely fine, but the doctor asked, 'Is he allergic to school?'

Every day opened with mental arithmetic, and I couldn't do it. I'd just blurt out the first thing that came into my head. I would be wrong, so of course I would be caned straight away. Then I could relax, because after mental arithmetic there was spelling and I could spell like a champion. I just got the idea that you were caned and punished as part of life.

Then we had psychological abuse in the form of hell. We were told our souls were eternally black. I can't tell you, Leigh, how much my mind was screwed up. By the time I got to seventeen I didn't know whether I was Arthur or Martha, or whether I was Catholic or non-Catholic. I was definitely going to go to hell, there was no question about that. It was only a matter of when. My soul was perpetually black.

And you say the guilt and psychological trauma of this has continued through your life to this day—and you're now seventy-two?
Absolutely. You never get over it; you never recover from all the guilt. However, I also want to make the point that Christ never talked like that.

That's my next question. How on earth did we get from Christ to that?
Yeah. 'Love one another.' The Sermon on the Mount is extraordinary, as are all the things that you read Christ said. So how is it that the Catholic Church thought it was OK to flog and psychologically and sexually abuse kids? How could that have happened?

I wonder, then, how you ended up in the education system as a teacher.
I often think about that because there was nothing about school that was appealing. However, I do remember one man, Brother Joseph, who asked me one day to look after a fourth class. I got a real buzz out of that. Balance is really important in all of this, and in amongst the hideousness there was Brother Joseph. He simply said, 'You did really well.' That could have been it.

I want to return to the issue of music for children. From your wealth of experience, how should schools and parents be connecting kids with music?

The way to music for every child is through singing. You don't need an instrument. You need to start with the voice. Singing is how children learn all the musical concepts. They learn rhythm, pitch, harmony. They also learn to memorise; they learn text, patterns and composition. They learn to improvise and accompany themselves with instruments. So when they get to learning an instrument, all that groundwork is done.

The reason so many children give up instruments is too much information has to be taught at once. We're not asking parents to pitch in millions of dollars for instruments. There is a human voice there already.

Which leads me to your grand passion for opera, in which you've held numbers of significant roles. What it is about opera and the music of opera that so captivates you?

Opera is a walking disaster! Of all the musical styles, nothing is more difficult than opera. You are dealing with characters whose entire output depends on a tiny muscle in their throats. Multiply that by the number of people in the cast and you've got a kindergarten on your hands, plus a room full of divas. You've also got an orchestra having the same sorts of issues!

It's irresistible because when you're standing in the pit and the orchestra is there and the performers are on stage and it's powering on, it's one of the most exciting things in the whole world. My role is to encourage them to do their best. You get great performances from people—that's what I love.

Can I ask you briefly about two specific musical experiences out of thousands? First from opera, which provides quite an insight into how ruthless and just plain bitchy this 'wonderful world of music' can be. It concerns one particular performance of Turandot.
I was conducting *Turandot* for the Australian Opera. [The role of] Turandot was being sung by a really special diva named Leona Mitchell, a wonderful, wonderful singer. It was in the second act, one of the most difficult arias in the repertoire. I turned over the page in the score and it wasn't there! The aria was not there—it had been lifted from my score!

Somebody had pinched it deliberately?
Yes, quite neatly. It's like letting your life jacket run out of air at the crucial point of the act. I was panicked out of my mind, but I had to let this diva know that everything was just fine! If you were going to hope that a conductor would fall on his face, that's what you'd take.

So why would someone have taken it?
I can only think jealously. It's just how it is. It wasn't a loose leaf, not something that fell out of the score. Now I always take my scores with me—I never leave them in the pit!

Second musical experience: David Helfgott's first main public outing. You were the conductor. What was the process and the performance like?
Well, you've got to love David Helfgott! There is no question about his extraordinary musical ability and his fantastic memory. When he came into the room for our first rehearsal, he had who knows how many cigarettes and cups of coffee in his hands.

We started to rehearse and I honestly wondered whether we would ever get there.

It came to the night of the concert and I'd opened the program with the Puccini Gloria Mass. I saw Helfgott walking away from the stage heading out the back of the concert hall towards the river! I raced up and said, 'David, David, we've got to get ready.' I walked him to the entrance of the stage and shoved him on and the house went wild. You've never heard anything like it.

The first movement was spectacular; the second movement was really lyrical and beautiful. We'd had discussions about the speed of the third movement because he wanted to go like the clappers. He started the third movement and he knew there was nothing I could do about it. He just went like the wind. I looked over at one of the bass players and she looked at me as if to say, 'He gotcha!' So we kept up.

It was extraordinary. The house went mad. It was an unbelievable night.

Richard, notwithstanding all the inevitable slings and arrows that you've experienced—that anyone would during a lifetime of music, education and performance—what has kept you going through all of it?
Trying to do it properly. I sweat every note of every concert I'm about to do. The most important thing for me about music is the music. Whereas I was motivated early in my life about me, I couldn't care less about fifteen minutes of fame now. I do care, however, about how the music goes.

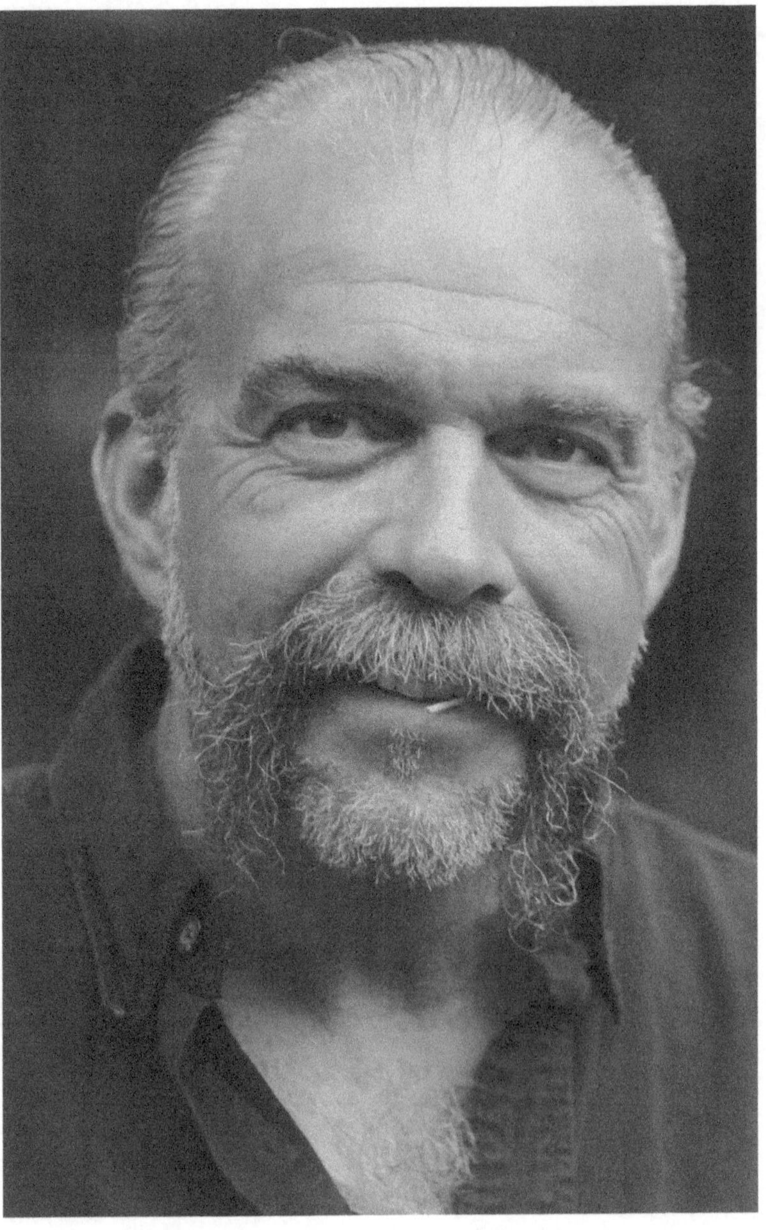

Sam Childers

'Machine Gun Preacher'

Sam Childers is a former drug-dealing criminal and bikie gang member. He's lived a life so incredible that a Hollywood movie has been made about it. Sam is known as the Machine Gun Preacher.

Through much of Sam's early life, his father repeatedly predicted that he was going to be killed. Eventually Sam started to believe him and became worried. Then came a simply astonishing transformation.

Sam sought to re-establish his relationship with God and then found an unexpected calling: to be the saviour of hundreds of kidnapped and orphaned children. We must warn that there are graphic, disturbing images in this interview.

Sam built an orphanage in Southern Sudan—and stood up to the notorious 'Lord's Resistance Army', leading armed missions to rescue children. Sixteen years later the orphanage he started is the largest in Southern Sudan. It has fed and housed over one thousand children. As Sam explained to us, it's all a very long way from those early years.

I was always fighting. The odds were always against me. I always felt that if you were going to get into a fight, it wasn't going to be a fight unless it was with somebody bigger than you. All my life I was always fighting for someone else. I could never stand people picking on others. I'd always go after them.

Sam, tell us where that all led you through those early years.
At a very young age I started doing drugs. I was raised in the perfect family. Born-again Christian, Spirit-filled; had a little bit of money. But at eleven years old I made, of my own free will, some bad decisions—smoking cigarettes, smoking marijuana at age thirteen, experimenting with alcohol and doing pills. All of a sudden at fifteen years old it wasn't cool any more, but I didn't care and I started putting a needle in my arm. I started selling drugs. Then I became a hired gun at drug deals.

I went as deep and as far as you could go into the darkness. But one thing I can say is that my mum and dad never quit praying for me. I know now that God never stopped loving me. Christ never stopped loving me. No matter what I did, he always loved me—but I walked away from him.

That's big love, isn't it?
Yes, absolutely.

Based on what you were like and what you did, your dad's words started to come back to haunt you.
Yes. I was living in Orlando, Florida. To be honest with you, I never had a problem with dying—I still don't—but I have a problem with what I'm going to die for. If I'm going to die for something stupid, something that's not worth dying for, I don't like that. So I got into a bad bar fight in Florida and I almost got killed. It turned out to be a shootout. On the way home that night I thought to myself,

'I'm done living this lifestyle.' I went home and told my wife Lynne that we were moving. She was excited because she was ready for a change.

She had a rough background too. She was raised in a Christian home, but around fifteen or sixteen years old she started experimenting with drugs and alcohol. I actually met my wife at a drug deal when she was working as a stripper in a strip joint.

We moved back to Pennsylvania and straight away my wife started going to church.

As she was going to church, what were you saying to her and what were you thinking?

I was hard on her for a couple of years. She'd come home from church and she'd be all fired up for God. You could just see it all over her—she was glowing. I would start cussing her because I was angry that she was happy when inside I was still miserable.

Then one night I woke up in the middle of the night and I could feel a presence in the room. There was this fear that just came over me. I literally started shaking in the bed because I was so scared. My wife was at the foot of the bed praying for me. She was praying out, screaming out to God and speaking in tongues and just saying, 'God, you've got to change this man.' I laid there and I shook. The fear of God was upon me and the presence of God was in that room.

It was about two weeks later that I said to her, 'All right, I'll go to church with you.' That first night I was chained to the pew! I had chains on my feet and chains on my hands—I just wouldn't get up. Then the preacher came walking right down the aisle up to me in the back seat and says, 'Man, the power of God is all over you—what's your problem?' I broke in the back seat of that church that night.

I went back the next night. I wanted what I felt in that back row, but I knew if I got closer to the front it would be better. So I went to the front seat. I said, 'God, here I am—it's all yours, use me.' Lots of times as Christians we only give God a little bit. We don't give him everything. No matter how messed up you are, if you give God everything, he'll start straightening it out.

I don't suppose that you could have possibly imagined where that request to God would lead.
When I think back to June of 1992, when this all started, I would never have dreamed that all of this would be happening today.

So how did this 'call' to go to Southern Sudan come to you?
It started when a preacher prophesied over my mum before she even conceived me that her next child was going to be a preacher and speak to the nations. Then, when I was five or six years old, there was a prophecy when my mum was standing at an altar, holding me by the hand, that her son was going to be a preacher. By the time I was eighteen she thought they were all liars! But one thing about my mum, she never stopped praying. I tell people all the time, 'You've got to remember that prophecy is real. If God speaks it, it will happen!'

And it was the body of a child torn apart by a landmine that drew you to Sudan.
I had gone there on a five-week mission trip. It changed my life. I stood over the body of a small child, probably just a year or two old, and I said, 'God, how can this happen?' This child had stepped on a landmine. How could this happen around the world and we not hear about it? Right now, as we speak, in Darfur there's a child

dying every four minutes. I said, 'God, I'll do whatever it takes to help these people.'

I went back to Sudan about a year-and-a-half later and started supporting the people pulling landmines out. The next thing, I started up a mobile clinic. Then all of a sudden I'm driving through the jungle one day and God stops me, right in the middle of the jungle, and says, 'This is where I want the children's village.' It was in the middle of a war zone where Joseph Kony and the Lord's Resistance Army were active. So I started this children's village. I just kept rescuing children who'd been kidnapped as child soldiers. We've rescued over one thousand children.

And you go out searching for these kids with your machine gun?
We would go out with the government soldiers into the bush where there were 'hot areas', where people were being attacked and killed. We would go out into villages and find these children hiding out, but we'd often be ambushed. These are children ranging from new-born right up to fifteen or sixteen-year-olds.

Tell us about the dangers you've experienced there.
Let me tell you I've never really felt the danger. I have been shot at many times, but I've probably been in more gunfights in the US than in Sudan!

But let me tell you what the rebels do. They will do everything from cutting the lips off children to cutting off their arms and legs to nailing them to trees. Some of the soldiers will actually take little babies by the ankles and bust their heads on trees—just unbelievable things.

I've had people say, 'How can you as a preacher go out and pick up a gun and rescue these children?' What I always ask is,

'How can you as a Christian stand by and let it happen?' Definitely Jesus Christ does not condone violence. But I don't believe that he condones children being nailed to a tree either.

The orphanage you built meant a great deal of personal sacrifice for you.
Yes, a lot of sacrifice. There was a time when I literally laid it all on the line and gave up all my personal stuff just to make it happen. I sold boats, campers, motorcycles, my gun collection—everything I had in the US.

Over there you slept under a mosquito net with a Bible in one hand and an AK47 in the other.
When it first started. I slept on a grass mat and I had a Bible on one side and a machine gun on the other side. That was how you had to do it.

How close have you come to being killed?
Many, many times. When bullets whiz by your head, that's pretty close! I don't ever really think of that or end up counting how many times.

I think the biggest thing in the world today is to concentrate on what we *haven't* done rather than on what we've done. Right now I've got an AIDS orphanage and a school I've built in Ethiopia, where we feed 165 kids a day. I've got two bases in Uganda and a school where I feed 770 kids a day. We feed a total of about 3500 meals a day. People think that's just great. But I can't focus on what little good I've done because then that slows us up for doing any more.

And when someone came to you and said, 'We want to make a movie out of this story', what was that like for you?
If it had happened like that I would have just fallen over!

It began with *Dateline NBC* doing a story on the Lord's Resistance Army and Joseph Kony in 2004. When they came into Sudan I was going to do some security work for them, and they said, 'Are you this guy everyone is calling the machine gun preacher? Man, we want to switch our story around and do the story on you!' That came out in 2005 and showed the world who I was. Our website crashed overnight! Everybody and their brother was emailing us, wanting to do a documentary, a book, a movie on my life.

The movie is doing unbelievably. When the DVDs hit the shelves here in Australia, within a couple of days it was the second best seller. Now I believe it's the top seller. Do you realise that it's the number one pirated movie in the world right now? It's been pirated off the internet over fifty-one million times!

I tell you why I'm excited about it, because people finding out about me see that God is still in the miracle-working business. Just in the last few weeks in Australia we've had over 3200 people come to the Lord at our meetings. In just the last year we've had over 15,000 lives around the world changed by the message of hope. That's awesome—the movie is doing amazing things.

So, Sam, when you look at those children you're helping, considering where they've come from and where they are now—what do you feel?
For me now I'm more concentrating on their future. We're going to be able to send them to university and they'll be able to learn a trade, working in the businesses that we have. The biggest thing is that you're teaching those children how to live in the future. So I can't really look at any good I've done in the past. You've got to concentrate on the future in everything.

For details on Sam Childers and the movie go to <www.machinegunpreacher.org>.

openhouse
openhouse
openhouse

Ken Duncan

Panoramic prince

Ken Duncan says he's 'just an average photographer with a great God'—an interpreter of God's creation.

Ken was born to missionary parents serving in the Kimberley and there began a deep, emotional and spiritual relationship with that beautiful region of Australia, as well as with many other iconic Australian scenes.

He's carved out an enviable international career with his stunning panoramic photography, which has probably left one of his school teachers somewhat surprised!

When I left school, my teacher told me I would be the least likely person to succeed he had ever met. I thought, 'Thanks for the encouragement!' However, at age sixteen I was taking photographs, and when I first saw a black and white photo come up in a processing tray, it was like an epiphany. I saw that I could take pictures that could tell a story. I realised the power of that, and it was probably to the detriment of all my school work because I became obsessed with photography.

Then I went off and turned my love into a money-making thing —selling photographic equipment rather than taking photographs.

I amassed all these possessions that are meant to make people happy and it wasn't working for me.

Then all of a sudden we found out about these panoramic cameras, and I took one on a surfing trip to Bali. When I came back and saw these photos of creation, I thought, 'This is what I want to do.' I just decided, 'That's it, I'm leaving my job.' I was three months away from long-service leave, but it didn't matter: I just wanted to go back to the Kimberley with my dad, who was going back to spend time with the Aboriginals. I thought, 'I'm going off with this new camera and I have to find meaning to life—there has to be more than what I'm doing.'

A very important part of your journey was the way you were nurtured by Australia's Indigenous community and your very deep connection with them.

They were very gracious to me because of my dad and they put up with me. They tolerated me, I think! On one trip into the bush we were looking for this cave. I was constantly saying to this old Aboriginal fella, 'So how far is it?'

He says, 'Oh, little bit long way, maybe one jump up, maybe two' (a 'jump up' is a hill.) So we go up four or five more hills and I would say again, 'So how far now?'

He would go, 'Oh, little bit long way.'

This went on for days: 'little bit long way, one jump up, maybe two.' Then finally I lost it. I said, 'Look, you've been telling me about all these jump ups and whatever. Hello—how far is this cave?' He just looked at me and said, 'Does it really matter? Shouldn't the journey be just as important as the destination?'

That messed with my mind, but I started to relax. I started to forget about when we were going to get there. Now he started telling me, 'You've got to learn to feel the land.' I was just beginning to make sense of what was happening.

This is why I'm 'an average photographer with a great God'. Often I'm out there thinking, 'God, what are we doing down here? Can you just give me a bit of help?' He has never let me down. So it's actually about being out of control and relaxing.

And learning about time.

Yes, letting go of that. The thought of 'control' for us is laughable really. We're on a planet travelling 108,000 kilometres per hour hurtling through space. For a side salad I think we are rotating at 1700 kilometres per hour. Here is a little human on earth saying, 'I'm in control! I'm in control!' If God puts the brakes on, man, you'll see how much control you've got!

Did you ever find the cave?

Look, we didn't at that time, but it was so funny because I was there with my dad and this Christian man, Howard Coates. He was a missionary and biblical scholar, and he would keep talking to me. I was arguing because I was anti-Christian, but he knew the Bible so well that he would blow me away. Every argument I ever had just wouldn't stand up.

So we got to this valley and I knew that the cave was in that valley. However, we had simply run out of time. It took us weeks to walk into this area, but we were living off the land and we had to get back out.

Then about five years ago, Howard went back in and found the cave. It was a significant cave called Grey's Cave. Eventually I followed, flying in by helicopter—a lot easier than walking, I can tell you! We went into the cave and there was a bottle that Howard had left, and he'd left a note inside. It said, 'Ken, I know you'll get here and it was exactly where we thought it was!'

How many years had elapsed?
It was about twenty-five years. I was in tears because that man had a real impact on my life because he loved me. I was no Christian by any means, but he didn't judge me. This man's faith was not in the world, his faith was in God. He was so respected by the Aboriginals. The cave was not the important thing. The important thing was spending that time with Howard and my dad and the Aboriginals, learning to humble myself.

And the faith that he nurtured in you opened your eyes more broadly to creation.
If you want to be truly creative, get to know the Creator. God is always about taking us way beyond our comfort zones. Comfort is the biggest killer on a spiritual journey.

For instance, I was very comfortable photographing Australia. Then one morning, 3.00 am (I was a Christian by this stage), God gave me a message: 'If America abandons "In God We Trust" from their money, I will abandon them as a nation.' I'm thinking: 'God, you're talking to the wrong person. I'm Ken Duncan, "Australia wide". It's the perfect time to talk to Americans—they're all awake over there right now. You should talk to one of them.'

But the next morning I woke up and got the thought that God wanted me to do a book on all fifty states of America, for them to get their focus back on the God they say they trust. So I went off to do that. But I needed a million dollars. I talked to various publishers and they said, 'Yes, we'll do the book.' But I had a specific title in mind, *America Wide—In God We Trust*, and all of them said, 'Look, we can't really have the God factor because it's politically incorrect.' So they wouldn't fund it.

I said, 'Well, that's non-negotiable, because otherwise it will just be another boring book of pictures.' They said, 'How are you going to do it then?' I said, 'Well, I've got a big God—I'll do it myself!'

Anyhow, we did end up doing it. When I came back to my wife, we put everything on the line again, which constantly seems to be my journey. She said, 'We don't own anything, God owns it, so what's the problem?'

The stunning part of this story is how it all ended up.
Yes. John Howard found out about the book and asked if he could grab a copy to give to George Bush as a gift from Australia. And very unusually, he allowed me to write a letter with the book. So I wrote: 'Mr Bush, the reason I have done this book is to remind America of the God they say they trust, because that is the only thing that will hold you strong through the troubled times ahead.' That book was given to George Bush the day before the September 11 attacks.

George Bush wrote back to me later and said, 'Ken, thank you. At a time when I have had to make some of the most difficult decisions, I would sit and look upon the beauty of my nation and be reminded of what an awesome God we serve.'

Ken, when I hear your story and what you have done in your life, I am left to conclude you have to be one of the most patient men in the world, especially when it comes to photography.
I think God allowed me to be a landscape photographer because I had to deal with patience. I was one of those impatient people. God's got a bigger picture in life.

You will sometimes wait for hours, even days, for the right light for the right shot.
Yes, because it's all about the moment. And it's fun waiting. I think sometimes God keeps me waiting because he likes to spend time with me. You don't have to get religious. I believe if you humble yourself in nature, you will sense his presence. You will start to see the patterns of the weather and things all of a sudden evolve, and when that moment happens—bang, you're on it!

I'd love you to tell to us about one of your grand passions: your 'Walk a While' project.
Indigenous people have this philosophy that says, 'If you really want to know me, you need to be prepared to walk a while with me.' That's what my dad did up in the Kimberly as a missionary. He didn't go up there to bash them over the head with a Bible. He went there to teach them skills in mustering cattle and things like that and show his Christianity in who he was.

So for the last seven or eight years we've been working out in the outback in creative arts. We're trying to set up an arts centre for photography, cinematography and music making so we can go out there and walk a while with them to educate some of the new generation. We've got some greatly talented people who have offered to come and help us. Any person who comes out there to walk with these people is going to get more blessed than the blessing they're leaving behind them.

So it comes down to people with whatever gifts or talents they've got. I'd love to have you out there, Leigh, because you could teach them how to do this radio thing.

I'd love to! Ken, can I put to you one quote that I read of yours about where you work: 'The vast emptiness of these landscapes does something to people. Nature has the ability to unmask you and people are often scared of that.'
They are—people are scared of facing themselves and their own fears, and that's what nature does. We need to get connected back to nature. It's not scary; it's the opposite. When I look at the stars I don't think, 'Look at all those stars—they're going to fall on me!' I think, 'Wow! If God can create them, there's nothing impossible for him.'

So why do you think creation sometimes scares people?
Because it makes you realise how small you are. But then you can really see how big God is.

I think it's interesting that your vision has not only transformed you personally but also been a great commercial success.
God has blessed us, but any money we make we end up spending again on doing a new project. My wife has a real heart to give too. If I get upstairs with a million dollars in my bank account, God's not going to be impressed with that at all. He's going to say, 'Why didn't you use that money while you were on earth to change lives?' I think there are too many people who think money is what it's all about. If you've got lots of money, that's fantastic—but make sure you use it wisely on earth to benefit people other than yourself.

With all these things comes responsibility. Mahatma Gandhi said: 'There is enough in this world for every man's need, but not for every man's greed.'

About Leigh Hatcher

Leigh Hatcher has had a distinguished career in broadcast journalism for four decades. He began working at Radio 2GB in Sydney and in 1975 was appointed to Canberra where he covered the Whitlam constitutional crisis for the Macquarie Network.

He was appointed news editor of Radio 2CA in Canberra, then news editor and program director of Radio 5DN in Adelaide, before moving to television with the Seven Network in the Canberra press gallery.

He went on to work for two years in London as the European correspondent for the Seven Network and returned to 5DN to host its news-talk breakfast program. Through the '90s Leigh worked as an on-the-road reporter, newsreader and chief Olympic correspondent for the Seven Network in Sydney.

In 1997 he took a year off work to study theology full time at Moore Theological College.

For thirteen years he worked as a senior presenter on Sky News, and he took over *Open House* from its founder, Sheridan Voysey, in May 2011. He also wrote his first book for the radio program, *Open House: A new era with Leigh Hatcher*, in 2012.

Leigh is the author of *I'm Not Crazy, I'm Just a Little Unwell*, the best-selling account of his two years in the wilderness of chronic fatigue syndrome from 1998 to 2000.

Leigh is married to Meredith and they have four children—Tristan, Amy, Johanna and Sophie. He also has three gorgeous grandsons, Reuben, Nathan and Daniel. In his spare time Leigh chills out with his long-term hobby of bonsai. He also plays bass, drums and jazz guitar (though not all at once). When he grows up, he wants to be a rock star!

Join the Conversation

Leigh Hatcher's *Open House* program can be heard on a network of Christian and family radio stations around Australia every Sunday night from 8 pm to 11 pm EST. The *Open House* network stretches from Hobart to Darwin, Melbourne, Sydney, Adelaide and Perth, as well as Canberra, the Gold Coast, the Riverland, Wollongong and on the Vision Radio Network.

The Open House Community website (www.openhousecommunity.com.au) has all the latest details and podcasts of the program, and a vibrant conversation is always underway on the Open House Community Facebook page.

Follow Leigh on Twitter @LeighHatcher.